JUMBLE®

SEE & SEARCH ™ 2

Back and Better Than Ever

SEE THE JUMBLE®

SEARCH THE PICTURE

FIND ALL THE FUN

David L. Hoyt and Jeff Knurek

TRIUMPH
BOOKS

This book is available in quantity at special discounts
for your group or organization. For further information, contact:

Triumph Books
814 North Franklin Street
Chicago, Illinois 60610
(800) 888-4741

Printed in U.S.A.
Cover design by Jeff Knurek.

ISBN-13: 978-1-57243-734-0
ISBN-10: 1-57243-734-0

CONTENTS

Star Bonus Puzzles

Two-in-One Puzzles

Three-in-One Puzzles

Busy, Busy, Busy Puzzles

Photo Jumble® Puzzles

What's Different? Puzzles

Answers

JUMBLE®
SEE & SEARCH™

★ Star ★ Bonus

LOTS OF JUMBLES®
ONE MYSTERY ANSWER AND
A BONUS MYSTERY OBJECT
EVERY ANSWER HAS SOMETHING
TO DO WITH THE PICTURE

We've put a lot of Jumbles® in each puzzle with one Jumble®
mystery answer and one bonus mystery object. Can you find
all the Jumbles® in the picture? Can you solve the mystery answer?

Unscramble the mixed up letters to make words. If you get
stumped, look at the picture. Each and every answer has something
to do with the picture … all you have to do is find it. Some Jumbles®
are verbs and are shown with the symbol 🍎. Other Jumbles® are
adjectives and are shown with this symbol: 🍎.

You'll be solving one Jumble® mystery answer plus a bonus object in the
"STAR BONUS" puzzles. You'll have to look at the picture for help. As
with all Jumble® See & Search™ puzzles, all the answers can be found
in the picture.

EVERY ANSWER HAS SOMETHING TO DO WITH THE PICTURE

#1 **EUTB**

CLUE   The street artist knew how to do this.

MYSTERY
ANSWER   ⬡⬡⬡⬡⬡ **A** ⬡⬡⬡⬡⬡⬡

BONUS
MYSTERY
OBJECT   ★★★★★

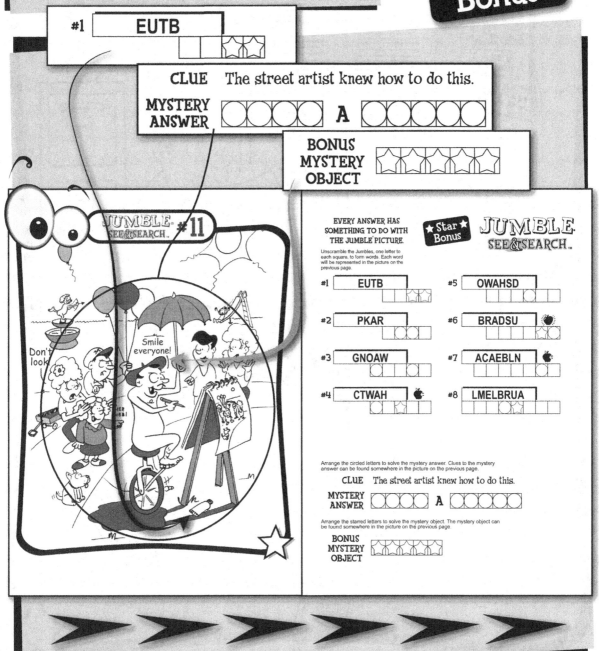

Don't look

Smile everyone!

JUMBLE® SEE&SEARCH™ #11

EVERY ANSWER HAS
SOMETHING TO DO WITH
THE JUMBLE PICTURE.   ★ Star ★ Bonus   JUMBLE® SEE&SEARCH™

Unscramble the Jumbles, one letter to
each square, to form words. Each word
will be represented in the picture on the
previous page.

#1   **EUTB**   #5   **OWAHSD**

#2   **PKAR**   #6   **BRADSU**

#3   **GNOAW**   #7   **ACAEBLN**

#4   **CTWAH**   #8   **LMELBRUA**

Arrange the circled letters to solve the mystery answer. Clues to the mystery
answer can be found somewhere in the picture on the previous page.

CLUE   The street artist knew how to do this.

MYSTERY
ANSWER   ⬡⬡⬡⬡ **A** ⬡⬡⬡⬡⬡

Arrange the starred letters to solve the mystery object. The mystery object can
be found somewhere in the picture on the previous page.

BONUS
MYSTERY
OBJECT   ★★★★★

1

EVERY ANSWER HAS
SOMETHING TO DO WITH
THE JUMBLE® PICTURE.

Unscramble the Jumbles, one letter to
each square, to form words. Each word
will be represented in the picture on the
previous page.

#1 LYLE

#2 RCDO

#3 KEDS

#4 YLZA

#5 HNCUL

#6 IKRDN

#7 LPHOSI

#8 BCETNIA

Arrange the circled letters to solve the mystery answer. Clues to the mystery
answer can be found somewhere in the picture on the previous page.

CLUE   The one thing the slacking secretary could file.

MYSTERY
ANSWER

Arrange the starred letters to solve the mystery object. The mystery object can
be found somewhere in the picture on the previous page.

BONUS
MYSTERY
OBJECT

3

EVERY ANSWER HAS
SOMETHING TO DO WITH
THE JUMBLE® PICTURE.

Unscramble the Jumbles, one letter to
each square, to form words. Each word
will be represented in the picture on the
previous page.

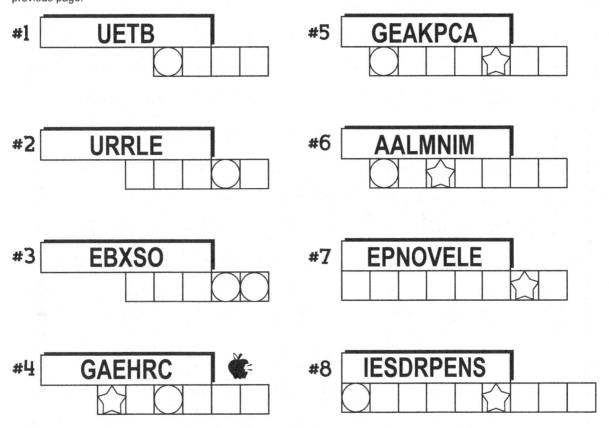

#1 UETB

#2 URRLE

#3 EBXSO

#4 GAEHRC

#5 GEAKPCA

#6 AALMNIM

#7 EPNOVELE

#8 IESDRPENS

Arrange the circled letters to solve the mystery answer. Clues to the mystery
answer can be found somewhere in the picture on the previous page.

CLUE   What the sale at the post office caused.

MYSTERY
ANSWER   A ◯◯◯◯◯◯◯◯

Arrange the starred letters to solve the mystery verb. The mystery verb can be
found somewhere in the picture on the previous page.

BONUS
MYSTERY
VERB   ☆☆☆☆☆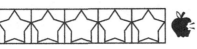

5

Unscramble the Jumbles, one letter to
each square, to form words. Each word
will be represented in the picture on the
previous page.

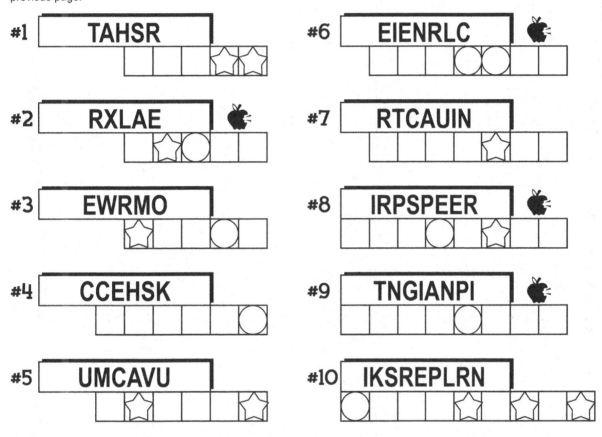

#1 TAHSR

#2 RXLAE

#3 EWRMO

#4 CCEHSK

#5 UMCAVU

#6 EIENRLC

#7 RTCAUIN

#8 IRPSPEER

#9 TNGIANPI

#10 IKSREPLRN

Arrange the circled letters to solve the mystery answer. Clues to the mystery
answer can be found somewhere in the picture on the previous page.

CLUE Completing all of the chores made him feel this way.

MYSTERY
ANSWER

Arrange the starred letters to solve the mystery objects. The mystery objects
can be found somewhere in the picture on the previous page.

BONUS
MYSTERY
OBJECTS

AND

JUMBLE.
SEE&SEARCH™

Unscramble the Jumbles, one letter to each square, to form words. Each word will be represented in the picture on the previous page.

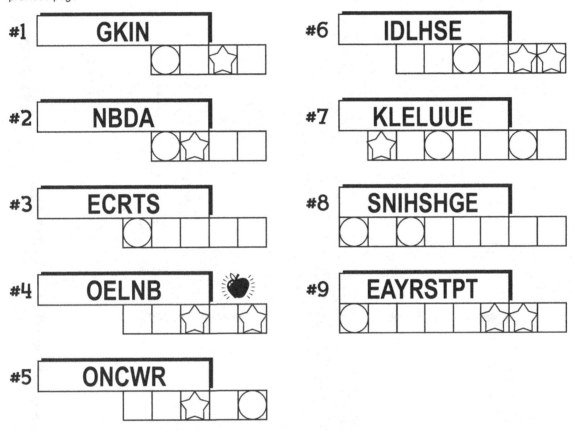

#1 GKIN

#2 NBDA

#3 ECRTS

#4 OELNB

#5 ONCWR

#6 IDLHSE

#7 KLELUUE

#8 SNIHSHGE

#9 EAYRSTPT

Arrange the circled letters to solve the mystery answer. Clues to the mystery answer can be found somewhere in the picture on the previous page.

CLUE   Where the royal guards went to relax.

MYSTERY ANSWER   AT A ◯◯◯◯◯◯◯ ◯◯◯◯

Arrange the starred letters to solve the mystery object. The mystery object can be found somewhere in the picture on the previous page.

BONUS MYSTERY OBJECT   ☆☆☆☆☆ ☆☆☆☆☆

EVERY ANSWER HAS
SOMETHING TO DO WITH
THE JUMBLE® PICTURE.

Unscramble the Jumbles, one letter to
each square, to form words. Each word
will be represented in the picture on the
previous page.

#1 EKCN

#2 EFLTU

#3 NABOJ

#4 OKKOY

#5 DTSNA

#6 IPDYALS

#7 SMUNCAII

#8 OAPONSHEX

#9 MTRSTIUNEN

Arrange the circled letters to solve the mystery answer. Clues to the mystery
answer can be found somewhere in the picture on the previous page.

CLUE   The guitarist was asked to leave because he was this.

MYSTERY
ANSWER

Arrange the starred letters to solve the mystery object. The mystery object can
be found somewhere in the picture on the previous page.

BONUS
MYSTERY
OBJECT

Unscramble the Jumbles, one letter to
each square, to form words. Each word
will be represented in the picture on the
previous page.

#1 SKAM

#2 FASN

#3 EHERC

#4 TOODCR

#5 LLSPAEC

#6 OCPNOPR

#7 PTEOREA

#8 FRIMNUO

#9 HLPSTOAI

Arrange the circled letters to solve the mystery answer. Clues to the mystery
answer can be found somewhere in the picture on the previous page.

CLUE   The ex-ball player did this when he became a surgeon.

MYSTERY
ANSWER   ⬡⬡⬡⬡ **THE** ⬡⬡⬡

Arrange the starred letters to solve the mystery object. The mystery object can
be found somewhere in the picture on the previous page.

BONUS
MYSTERY
OBJECT   ☆☆☆☆☆☆

13

★ Star ★ Bonus

Unscramble the Jumbles, one letter to each square, to form words. Each word will be represented in the picture on the previous page.

#1 KMLI

#2 LULB

#3 DNARB

#4 RCNUH

#5 TBOTEL

#6 OVHSOE

#7 LHEOLR

#8 CYSHAATK

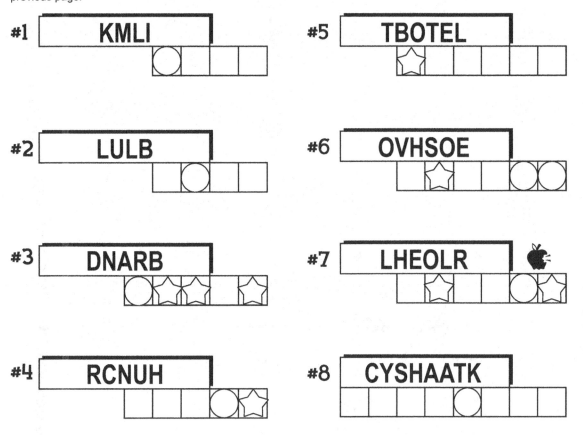

Arrange the circled letters to solve the mystery answer. Clues to the mystery answer can be found somewhere in the picture on the previous page.

CLUE   The cow wanted a divorce because she had this.

MYSTERY ANSWER   A ☐☐☐ ☐☐☐☐☐

Arrange the starred letters to solve the mystery object. The mystery object can be found somewhere in the picture on the previous page.

BONUS MYSTERY OBJECT   ☆☆☆☆ ☆☆☆

EVERY ANSWER HAS
SOMETHING TO DO WITH
THE JUMBLE® PICTURE.

Unscramble the Jumbles, one letter to
each square, to form words. Each word
will be represented in the picture on the
previous page.

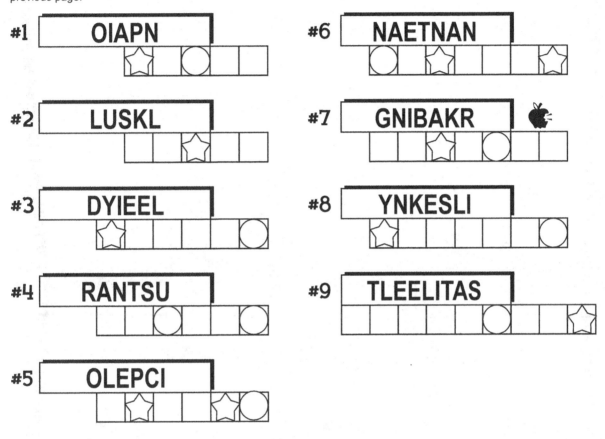

#1 OIAPN

#2 LUSKL

#3 DYIEEL

#4 RANTSU

#5 OLEPCI

#6 NAETNAN

#7 GNIBAKR

#8 YNKESLI

#9 TLEELITAS

Arrange the circled letters to solve the mystery answer. Clues to the mystery
answer can be found somewhere in the picture on the previous page.

CLUE   The lost space creature felt this way.

MYSTERY
ANSWER

Arrange the starred letters to solve the mystery object. The mystery object can
be found somewhere in the picture on the previous page.

BONUS
MYSTERY
OBJECT

17

Unscramble the Jumbles, one letter to
each square, to form words. Each word
will be represented in the picture on the
previous page.

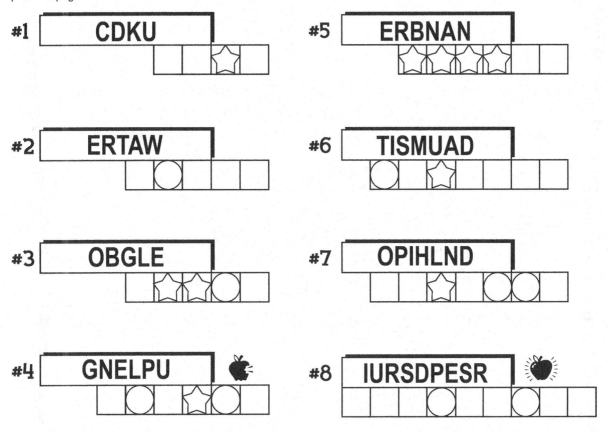

#1 CDKU

#2 ERTAW

#3 OBGLE

#4 GNELPU

#5 ERBNAN

#6 TISMUAD

#7 OPIHLND

#8 IURSDPESR

Arrange the circled letters to solve the mystery answer. Clues to the mystery
answer can be found somewhere in the picture on the previous page.

CLUE   What the novice Olympic diver made.

MYSTERY
ANSWER   A ⚪⚪⚪ ⚪⚪⚪⚪⚪⚪

Arrange the starred letters to solve the mystery object. The mystery object can
be found somewhere in the picture on the previous page.

BONUS
MYSTERY
OBJECT   ☆☆☆☆☆☆☆☆☆

19

Unscramble the Jumbles, one letter to
each square, to form words. Each word
will be represented in the picture on the
previous page.

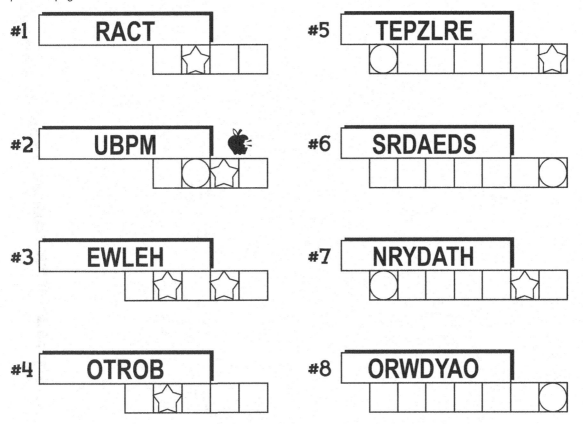

#1 RACT

#2 UBPM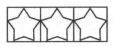

#3 EWLEH

#4 OTROB

#5 TEPZLRE

#6 SRDAEDS

#7 NRYDATH

#8 ORWDYAO

Arrange the circled letters to solve the mystery answer. Clues to the mystery
answer can be found somewhere in the picture on the previous page.

CLUE   They thought the street vendor was this.

MYSTERY
ANSWER   ○○○○○

Arrange the starred letters to solve the mystery object. The mystery object can
be found somewhere in the picture on the previous page.

BONUS
MYSTERY
OBJECT   ☆☆☆   ☆☆☆☆

21

EVERY ANSWER HAS
SOMETHING TO DO WITH
THE JUMBLE® PICTURE.

Unscramble the Jumbles, one letter to
each square, to form words. Each word
will be represented in the picture on the
previous page.

#1 EUTB

#5 OWAHSD

#2 PKAR

#6 BRADSU

#3 GNOAW

#7 ACAEBLN

#4 CTWAH

#8 LMELBRUA

Arrange the circled letters to solve the mystery answer. Clues to the mystery
answer can be found somewhere in the picture on the previous page.

CLUE   The street artist knew how to do this.

MYSTERY
ANSWER   ⬡⬡⬡⬡⬡ A ⬡⬡⬡⬡⬡⬡

Arrange the starred letters to solve the mystery object. The mystery object can
be found somewhere in the picture on the previous page.

Unscramble the Jumbles, one letter to
each square, to form words. Each word
will be represented in the picture on the
previous page.

#1 MILF

#2 LPNA

#3 ILAAV

#4 UMSOE

#5 KTSOEC

#6 ENLDEE

#7 IPGNSR

#8 IUNGSE

#9 REMAHM

#10 BYETRTA

Arrange the circled letters to solve the mystery answer. Clues to the mystery
answer can be found somewhere in the picture on the previous page.

CLUE   Inventing the light bulb guaranteed Edison one.

MYSTERY
ANSWER   A ◯◯◯◯◯◯◯   ◯◯◯◯◯◯◯

Arrange the starred letters to solve the mystery objects. The mystery objects
can be found somewhere in the picture on the previous page.

BONUS
MYSTERY
OBJECTS   ☆☆☆☆☆☆☆☆☆☆

25

26

EVERY ANSWER HAS
SOMETHING TO DO WITH
THE JUMBLE® PICTURE.

Unscramble the Jumbles, one letter to
each square, to form words. Each word
will be represented in the picture on the
previous page.

#1 **VEAW**

#2 **LGLU**

#3 **CYFNA**

#4 **RIMROR**

#5 **AERTWI**

#6 **ITOLON**

#7 **ELGUON**

#8 **PORWHSI**

#9 **OOSEPPIR**

Arrange the circled letters to solve the mystery answer. Clues to the mystery
answer can be found somewhere in the picture on the previous page.

CLUE   A conceited person's vacation can be this.

MYSTERY
ANSWER   **AN** ◯◯◯ ◯◯◯◯

Arrange the starred letters to solve the mystery object. The mystery object can
be found somewhere in the picture on the previous page.

BONUS
MYSTERY
OBJECT   ☆☆☆☆☆☆☆☆

27

Unscramble the Jumbles, one letter to
each square, to form words. Each word
will be represented in the picture on the
previous page.

#1 LGAF

#2 LIEP

#3 IHYFS

#4 ZOLEZN

#5 IRBGED

#6 CNORCAO

#7 CTHESN

#8 ENKRSSAE

#9 RSTAHACN

#10 OSSACMKKET

Arrange the circled letters to solve the mystery answer. Clues to the mystery
answer can be found somewhere in the picture on the previous page.

CLUE   The view at the dump was this.

MYSTERY
ANSWER

Arrange the starred letters to solve the mystery object. The mystery object can
be found somewhere in the picture on the previous page.

BONUS
MYSTERY
OBJECT

JUMBLE®
SEE&SEARCH™

★ Star ★
Bonus

Unscramble the Jumbles, one letter to each square, to form words. Each word will be represented in the picture on the previous page.

#1 OMBO

#2 OMCB

#3 EAYLL

#4 AITFN

#5 ETRTUG

#6 NWIXAG

#7 EWPDRO

#8 RSEFAM

#9 EABVGERE

#10 IRELDYVE

Arrange the circled letters to solve the mystery answer. Clues to the mystery answer can be found somewhere in the picture on the previous page.

CLUE   She was this when he said he loved her.

MYSTERY
ANSWER

Arrange the starred letters to solve the mystery object. The mystery object can be found somewhere in the picture on the previous page.

BONUS
MYSTERY
OBJECT

31

Unscramble the Jumbles, one letter to
each square, to form words. Each word
will be represented in the picture on the
previous page.

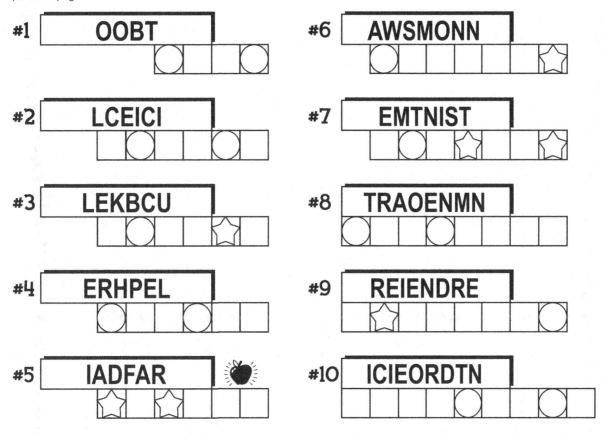

#1 OOBT

#2 LCEICI

#3 LEKBCU

#4 ERHPEL

#5 IADFAR

#6 AWSMONN

#7 EMTNIST

#8 TRAOENMN

#9 REIENDRE

#10 ICIEORDTN

Arrange the circled letters to solve the mystery answer. Clues to the mystery
answer can be found somewhere in the picture on the previous page.

CLUE   The child who is afraid of Santa is this.

MYSTERY
ANSWER

Arrange the starred letters to solve the mystery object. The mystery object can
be found somewhere in the picture on the previous page.

BONUS
MYSTERY
OBJECT

EVERY ANSWER HAS
SOMETHING TO DO WITH
THE JUMBLE® PICTURE.

Unscramble the Jumbles, one letter to
each square, to form words. Each word
will be represented in the picture on the
previous page.

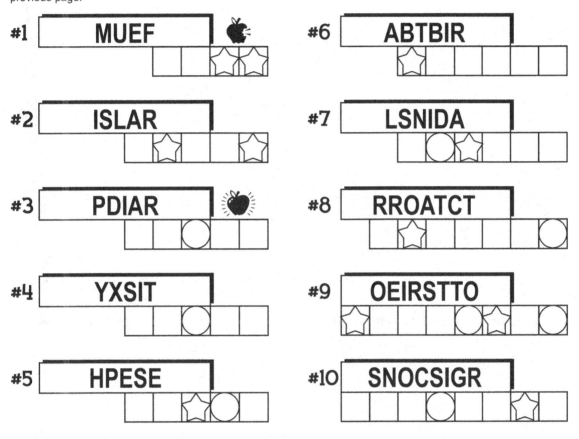

#1 MUEF

#2 ISLAR

#3 PDIAR

#4 YXSIT

#5 HPESE

#6 ABTBIR

#7 LSNIDA

#8 RROATCT

#9 OEIRSTTO

#10 SNOCSIGR

Arrange the circled letters to solve the mystery answer. Clues to the mystery
answer can be found somewhere in the picture on the previous page.

CLUE   A train conductor's favorite drink.

MYSTERY
ANSWER

Arrange the starred letters to solve the mystery object. The mystery object can
be found somewhere in the picture on the previous page.

BONUS
MYSTERY
OBJECT

Unscramble the Jumbles, one letter to
each square, to form words. Each word
will be represented in the picture on the
previous page.

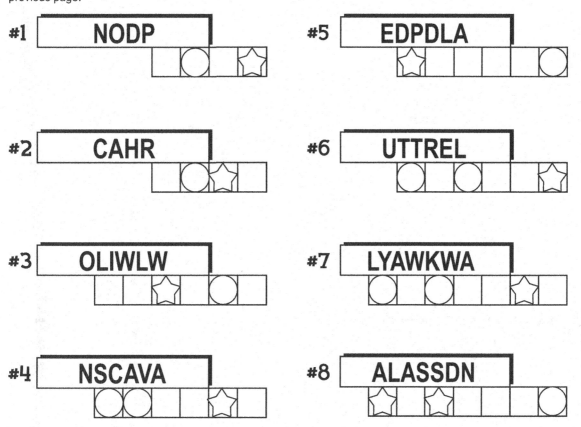

#1 NODP

#2 CAHR

#3 OLIWLW

#4 NSCAVA

#5 EDPDLA

#6 UTTREL

#7 LYAWKWA

#8 ALASSDN

Arrange the circled letters to solve the mystery answer. Clues to the mystery
answer can be found somewhere in the picture on the previous page.

CLUE   Blue and green are considered these.

MYSTERY
ANSWER

Arrange the starred letters to solve the mystery object. The mystery object can
be found somewhere in the picture on the previous page.

BONUS
MYSTERY
OBJECT

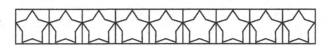

38

Unscramble the Jumbles, one letter to each square, to form words. Each word will be represented in the picture on the previous page.

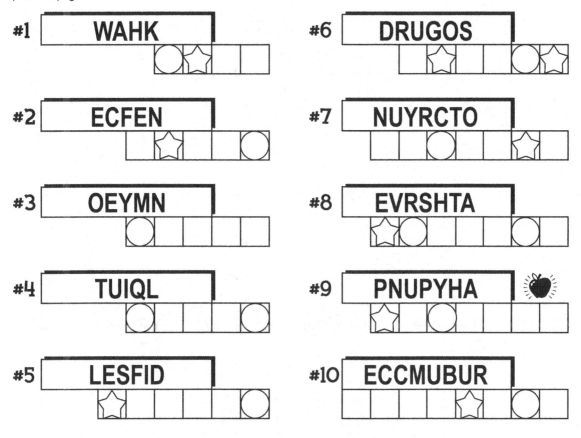

#1 WAHK

#2 ECFEN

#3 OEYMN

#4 TUIQL

#5 LESFID

#6 DRUGOS

#7 NUYRCTO

#8 EVRSHTA

#9 PNUPYHA

#10 ECCMUBUR

Arrange the circled letters to solve the mystery answer. Clues to the mystery answer can be found somewhere in the picture on the previous page.

CLUE   The successful farmer did this to his competition.

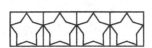

MYSTERY ANSWER

Arrange the starred letters to solve the mystery object. The mystery object can be found somewhere in the picture on the previous page.

BONUS MYSTERY OBJECT

EVERY ANSWER HAS
SOMETHING TO DO WITH
THE JUMBLE® PICTURE.

JUMBLE®
SEE&SEARCH™

Unscramble the Jumbles, one letter to
each square, to form words. Each word
will be represented in the picture on the
previous page.

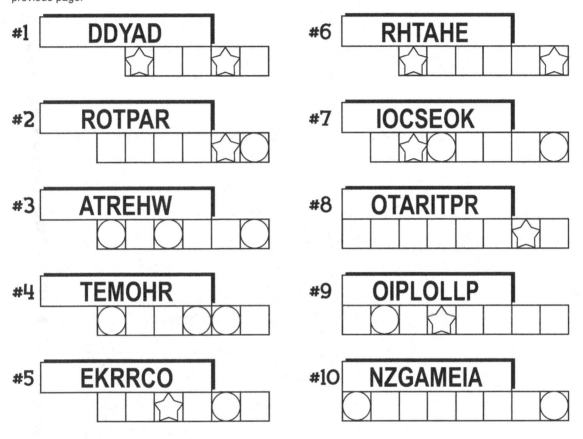

#1 DDYAD

#2 ROTPAR

#3 ATREHW

#4 TEMOHR

#5 EKRRCO

#6 RHTAHE

#7 IOCSEOK

#8 OTARITPR

#9 OIPLOLLP

#10 NZGAMEIA

Arrange the circled letters to solve the mystery answer. Clues to the mystery
answer can be found somewhere in the picture on the previous page.

CLUE   The grandchildren considered grandma's to be this.

MYSTERY
ANSWER

Arrange the starred letters to solve the mystery object. The mystery object can
be found somewhere in the picture on the previous page.

BONUS
MYSTERY
OBJECT

JUMBLE® SEE&SEARCH™

Unscramble the Jumbles, one letter to
each square, to form words. Each word
will be represented in the picture on the
previous page.

#1 **BUSLC**

#2 **UMDON**

#3 **LTWOE**

#4 **HAPSSL**

#5 **BKENUR**

#6 **KSPEIS**

#7 **CAEVDI**

#8 **RUBHSS**

#9 **GISWGNNI**

#10 **ICATNSDE**

Arrange the circled letters to solve the mystery answer. Clues to the mystery
answer can be found somewhere in the picture on the previous page.

CLUE   The persistent golfer had this.

MYSTERY
ANSWER

Arrange the starred letters to solve the mystery object. The mystery object can
be found somewhere in the picture on the previous page.

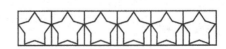

BONUS
MYSTERY
OBJECT

43

EVERY ANSWER HAS
SOMETHING TO DO WITH
THE JUMBLE® PICTURE.

Unscramble the Jumbles, one letter to
each square, to form words. Each word
will be represented in the picture on the
previous page.

#1 IXMES

#5 BTMOTO

#2 RUKND

#6 AEWDESE

#3 RKCEW

#7 ITRMANI

#4 ESLJWE

#8 AELHLESS

Arrange the circled letters to solve the mystery answer. Clues to the mystery
answer can be found somewhere in the picture on the previous page.

CLUE   The fish failed bartender school because his drinks
        were this.

MYSTERY
ANSWER

Arrange the starred letters to solve the mystery object. The mystery object can
be found somewhere in the picture on the previous page.

BONUS
MYSTERY
OBJECT

45

Unscramble the Jumbles, one letter to
each square, to form words. Each word
will be represented in the picture on the
previous page.

#1 RCBA

#2 CLIHL

#3 EMULP

#4 OBMABO

#5 TYORES

#6 EGNRES

#7 UPCOLE

#8 REEKSW

#9 OEPTIRNU

Arrange the circled letters to solve the mystery answer. Clues to the mystery
answer can be found somewhere in the picture on the previous page.

CLUE   A honeymoon salad is this.

MYSTERY
ANSWER

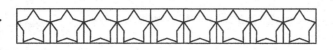

Arrange the starred letters to solve the mystery object. The mystery object can
be found somewhere in the picture on the previous page.

BONUS
MYSTERY
OBJECT

Unscramble the Jumbles, one letter to
each square, to form words. Each word
will be represented in the picture on the
previous page.

#1 LKYO

#2 OKZAO

#3 OLDYL

#4 SUBLH

#5 PTPEUP

#6 NOYRCA

#7 LEHTIWS

#8 RNLOSTI

#9 MAHDAES

#10 VSELESH

Arrange the circled letters to solve the mystery answer. Clues to the mystery
answer can be found somewhere in the picture on the previous page.

CLUE The naked toy was this.

**MYSTERY
ANSWER** A ⚪⚪⚪⚪⚪ ⚪⚪⚪⚪

Arrange the starred letters to solve the mystery object. The mystery object can
be found somewhere in the picture on the previous page.

**BONUS
MYSTERY
OBJECT**

JUMBLE.
SEE&SEARCH™

LOTS OF JUMBLES®
TWO DIFFERENT MYSTERY ANSWERS
EVERY ANSWER HAS SOMETHING
TO DO WITH THE PICTURE

We've put a lot of Jumbles® in each puzzle and put two different Jumble® mystery answers into the same picture. Can you find all the Jumbles® in the picture? Can you figure out which parts of the picture will help you solve the mystery answers?

Unscramble the mixed up letters to make words. If you get stumped, look at the picture. Each and every answer has something to do with the picture . . . all you have to do is find it. Some Jumbles® are verbs and are shown with the symbol 🍎. Other Jumbles® are adjectives and are shown with this symbol: 🍎.

You'll be solving two different Jumble® mystery answers in the "TWO-IN-ONE" puzzles. You'll have to look at the picture for help. Each mystery answer will correspond to part of the picture.

"TWO-IN-ONE" Jumble® See & Search™ is two times the fun.

JUMBLE® SEE&SEARCH™

Two-in-One

#2 ELHAW

#3 ORMOG

CLUE #2 The successful husband always got in the these last words.
MYSTERY ANSWER #2

JUMBLE SEE&SEARCH #31

It wasn't supposed to rain today!

You better make that rain stop!

TWO MYSTERY ANSWERS

EVERY ANSWER HAS SOMETHING TO DO WITH THE JUMBLE PICTURE

Two-in-One JUMBLE SEE&SEARCH™

Unscramble the Jumbles, one letter to each square, to form words. Each word will be represented in the picture on the previous page.

#1 HDIS

#2 ELHAW

#3 ORMOG

#4 OESOG

#5 RAWRO

#6 EDUTOX

#7 ARBERE

#8 RTMOSY

#9 ROCGAES

#10 NCUBODE

#11 GNLINTHIG

Arrange the circled letters to solve mystery answer #1. Arrange the diamonded letters to solve mystery answer #2. Clues to mystery answers can be found somewhere in the picture on the previous page.

CLUE #1 The bride wanted this before nuptials, not during.
MYSTERY ANSWER #1 A

CLUE #2 The successful husband always got in these last words.
MYSTERY ANSWER #2

Two-in-One JUMBLE. SEE & SEARCH™

Unscramble the Jumbles, one letter to each square, to form words. Each word will be represented in the picture on the previous page.

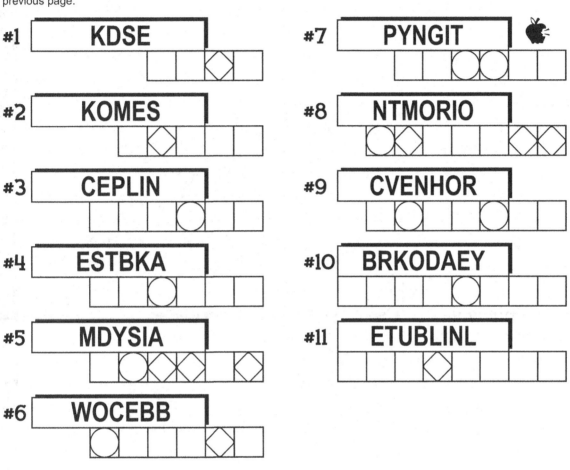

#1 KDSE

#2 KOMES

#3 CEPLIN

#4 ESTBKA

#5 MDYSIA

#6 WOCEBB

#7 PYNGIT

#8 NTMORIO

#9 CVENHOR

#10 BRKODAEY

#11 ETUBLINL

Arrange the circled letters to solve mystery answer #1. Arrange the diamonded letters to solve mystery answer #2. Clues to the mystery answers can be found somewhere in the picture on the previous page.

CLUE #1   A computer programmer's favorite snack.

MYSTERY ANSWER #1

CLUE #2   A sign that a computer is getting old.

MYSTERY ANSWER #2

EVERY ANSWER HAS
SOMETHING TO DO WITH
THE JUMBLE® PICTURE.

Two-in-One

JUMBLE®
SEE&SEARCH™

Unscramble the Jumbles, one letter to
each square, to form words. Each word
will be represented in the picture on the
previous page.

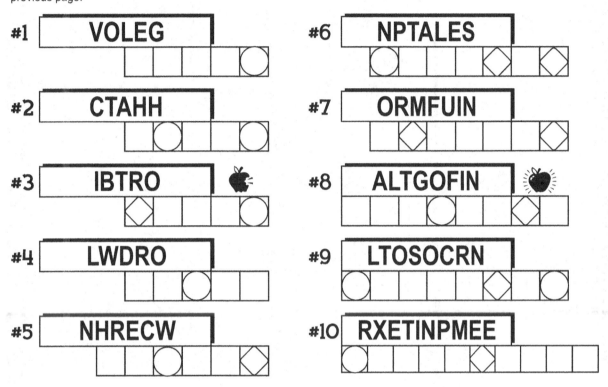

#1 VOLEG

#2 CTAHH

#3 IBTRO

#4 LWDRO

#5 NHRECW

#6 NPTALES

#7 ORMFUIN

#8 ALTGOFIN

#9 LTOSOCRN

#10 RXETINPMEE

Arrange the circled letters to solve mystery answer #1. Arrange the diamonded letters to solve mystery
answer #2. Clues to the mystery answers can be found somewhere in the picture on the previous page.

CLUE #1 The astronauts used one to warm up.

MYSTERY
ANSWER #1   A ◯◯◯◯◯ ◯◯◯◯◯◯

CLUE #2 An astronaut's favorite drink.

MYSTERY
ANSWER #2

EVERY ANSWER HAS
SOMETHING TO DO WITH
THE JUMBLE® PICTURE.

Unscramble the Jumbles, one letter to
each square, to form words. Each word
will be represented in the picture on the
previous page.

#1 LYCEC

#2 ENHPO

#3 RISUEC

#4 ERTAVL

#5 ATSUET

#6 AMRAEC

#7 DPIUMO

#8 ZAELBR

#9 CONIVATA

#10 ORSISCSS

#11 NIENRPSS

#12 IHMOCNPEOR

Arrange the circled letters to solve mystery answer #1. Arrange the diamonded letters to solve mystery
answer #2. Clues to the mystery answers can be found somewhere in the picture on the previous page.

CLUE #1 The game show player that would not stop talking was . . .
MYSTERY
ANSWER #1 AN

CLUE #2 The game show players tried to win this.
MYSTERY
ANSWER #2 A

EVERY ANSWER HAS
SOMETHING TO DO WITH
THE JUMBLE® PICTURE.

Two-in-One

JUMBLE®
SEE&SEARCH™

Unscramble the Jumbles, one letter to
each square, to form words. Each word
will be represented in the picture on the
previous page.

#1 LEBL

#2 LPIOWL

#3 UTACEF

#4 TEBKCU

#5 NEBVOI

#6 GSMAASE

#7 IPNUPMG

#8 LISDLIT

#9 NHCEIKC

#10 SRAKPEE

#11 EFYBTURTL

Arrange the circled letters to solve mystery answer #1. Arrange the diamonded letters to solve mystery
answer #2. Clues to the mystery answers can be found somewhere in the picture on the previous page.

CLUE #1 A pampered cow gives this.
MYSTERY
ANSWER #1

CLUE #2 A cow's favorite drink.
MYSTERY
ANSWER #2

59

Two-in-One JUMBLE.
SEE & SEARCH ™

Unscramble the Jumbles, one letter to
each square, to form words. Each word
will be represented in the picture on the
previous page.

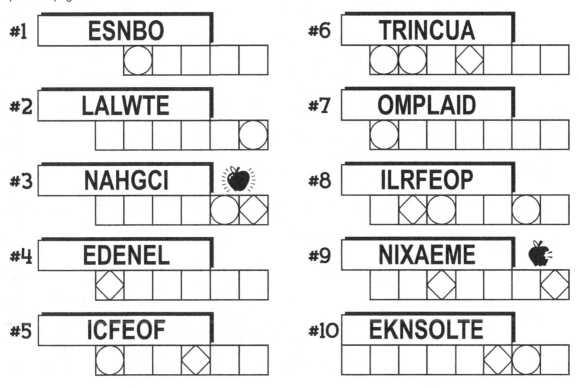

#1 **ESNBO**

#2 **LALWTE**

#3 **NAHGCI**

#4 **EDENEL**

#5 **ICFEOF**

#6 **TRINCUA**

#7 **OMPLAID**

#8 **ILRFEOP**

#9 **NIXAEME**

#10 **EKNSOLTE**

Arrange the circled letters to solve mystery answer #1. Arrange the diamonded letters to solve mystery
answer #2. Clues to the mystery answers can be found somewhere in the picture on the previous page.

CLUE #1   The vampire doctor's favorite test.

MYSTERY
ANSWER #1

CLUE #2   The doctor was doing this when he offered free services.

MYSTERY
ANSWER #2

EVERY ANSWER HAS
SOMETHING TO DO WITH
THE JUMBLE® PICTURE.

Unscramble the Jumbles, one letter to
each square, to form words. Each word
will be represented in the picture on the
previous page.

#1 APOS

#2 ONABC

#3 TRAEW

#4 VIGONL

#5 TEKNIT

#6 ASKDEO

#7 FETBUF

#8 SESLPIPR

#9 UNDTMOEC

#10 KHUFLNTA

Arrange the circled letters to solve mystery answer #1. Arrange the diamonded letters to solve mystery
answer #2. Clues to the mystery answers can be found somewhere in the picture on the previous page.

CLUE #1   The businessman wore one in the tub.

MYSTERY
ANSWER #1   A

CLUE #2   The children gave their sleeping mother this on her birthday.

MYSTERY
ANSWER #2   A

Unscramble the Jumbles, one letter to
each square, to form words. Each word
will be represented in the picture on the
previous page.

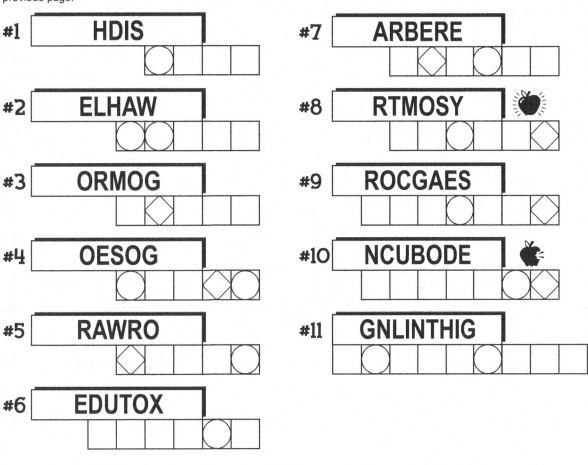

#1 HDIS

#2 ELHAW

#3 ORMOG

#4 OESOG

#5 RAWRO

#6 EDUTOX

#7 ARBERE

#8 RTMOSY

#9 ROCGAES

#10 NCUBODE

#11 GNLINTHIG

Arrange the circled letters to solve mystery answer #1. Arrange the diamonded letters to solve mystery
answer #2. Clues to the mystery answers can be found somewhere in the picture on the previous page.

CLUE #1   The bride wanted this before nuptials, not during.

MYSTERY
ANSWER #1   A ⬚⬚⬚⬚⬚⬚⬚   ⬚⬚⬚⬚⬚⬚

CLUE #2   The successful husband always got in these last words.

MYSTERY
ANSWER #2   ⬚⬚⬚   ⬚⬚⬚⬚

Two-in-One

JUMBLE®
SEE&SEARCH™

Unscramble the Jumbles, one letter to
each square, to form words. Each word
will be represented in the picture on the
previous page.

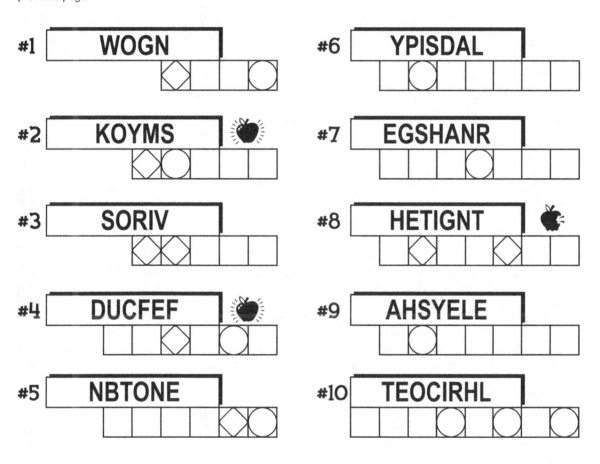

#1 WOGN

#2 KOYMS

#3 SORIV

#4 DUCFEF

#5 NBTONE

#6 YPISDAL

#7 EGSHANR

#8 HETIGNT

#9 AHSYELE

#10 TEOCIRHL

Arrange the circled letters to solve mystery answer #1. Arrange the diamonded letters to solve mystery
answer #2. Clues to the mystery answers can be found somewhere in the picture on the previous page.

CLUE #1 Searching for the perfect new ones can be one.
MYSTERY
ANSWER #1 A ⬡⬡⬡⬡⬡⬡ ⬡⬡⬡⬡

CLUE #2 A tempermental tailor can do this to his customers.
MYSTERY
ANSWER #2 ⬡⬡⬡⬡ THEM ⬡⬡⬡⬡

EVERY ANSWER HAS
SOMETHING TO DO WITH
THE JUMBLE PICTURE.

Two-in-One JUMBLE
SEE&SEARCH™

Unscramble the Jumbles, one letter to
each square, to form words. Each word
will be represented in the picture on the
previous page.

#1 PALFS

#2 KNESA

#3 OTEYCO

#4 OGTOHD

#5 LMTEEH

#6 FADIRA

#7 NGWIOHL

#8 ONKGOCI

#9 ODRUSTOO

#10 ICNOSPRO

Arrange the circled letters to solve mystery answer #1. Arrange the diamonded letters to solve mystery
answer #2. Clues to the mystery answers can be found somewhere in the picture on the previous page.

CLUE #1 What the fireman's ex-girlfriend was.
MYSTERY
ANSWER #1 AN ⬡⬡⬡ ⬡⬡⬡⬡⬡

CLUE #2 The campers got engaged near one.
MYSTERY
ANSWER #2 A ◇◇◇◇◇ OF ◇◇◇◇◇

69

EVERY ANSWER HAS
SOMETHING TO DO WITH
THE JUMBLE® PICTURE.

JUMBLE
SEE&SEARCH ™

Unscramble the Jumbles, one letter to
each square, to form words. Each word
will be represented in the picture on the
previous page.

#1 OIRN

#2 TAPSM

#3 EDNSUA

#4 ODNWIW

#5 REDBOR

#6 MFAILEN

#7 HOELCST

#8 IGALMOFN

#9 EHILNAED

#10 PERWNAPSE

Arrange the circled letters to solve mystery answer #1. Arrange the diamonded letters to solve mystery
answer #2. Clues to the mystery answers can be found somewhere in the picture on the previous page.

CLUE #1   He became one after telling his wife how to drive.

MYSTERY
ANSWER #1   A ◯◯◯◯◯◯◯◯◯◯◯

CLUE #2   Women get more love letters from him than anyone else.

MYSTERY
ANSWER #2   THE ◇◇◇◇◇◇◇

71

Unscramble the Jumbles, one letter to
each square, to form words. Each word
will be represented in the picture on the
previous page.

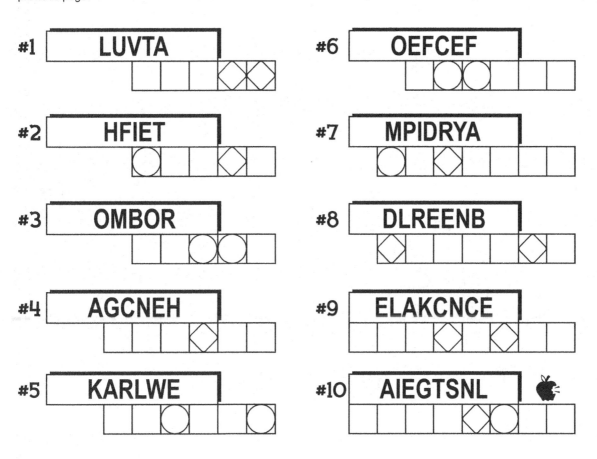

#1 LUVTA

#2 HFIET

#3 OMBOR

#4 AGCNEH

#5 KARLWE

#6 OEFCEF

#7 MPIDRYA

#8 DLREENB

#9 ELAKCNCE

#10 AIEGTSNL

Arrange the circled letters to solve mystery answer #1. Arrange the diamonded letters to solve mystery
answer #2. Clues to the mystery answers can be found somewhere in the picture on the previous page.

CLUE #1 The artistic investment banker showed off his.

MYSTERY
ANSWER #1

CLUE #2 When the cashier reported her coworker she was this.

MYSTERY
ANSWER #2 A

Two-in-One JUMBLE. SEE&SEARCH™

Unscramble the Jumbles, one letter to
each square, to form words. Each word
will be represented in the picture on the
previous page.

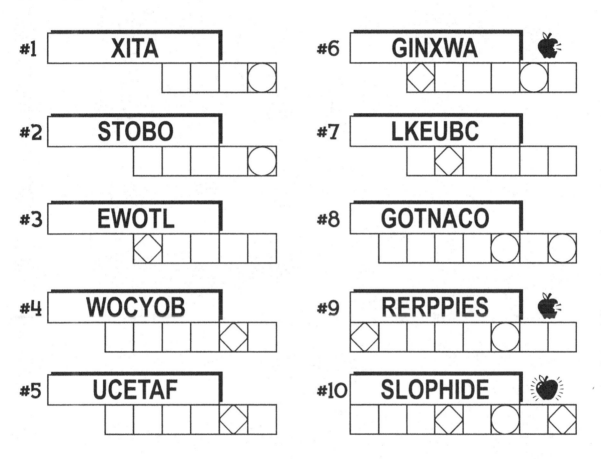

#1 XITA

#2 STOBO

#3 EWOTL

#4 WOCYOB

#5 UCETAF

#6 GINXWA

#7 LKEUBC

#8 GOTNACO

#9 RERPPIES

#10 SLOPHIDE

Arrange the circled letters to solve mystery answer #1. Arrange the diamonded letters to solve mystery
answer #2. Clues to the mystery answers can be found somewhere in the picture on the previous page.

CLUE #1   The top car washer set this type of example.

MYSTERY
ANSWER #1   A ⬡⬡⬡⬡⬡⬡ ONE

CLUE #2   The car-wash worker was this after a long day.

MYSTERY
ANSWER #2   ⬡⬡⬡⬡⬡ ⬡⬡⬡

75

Unscramble the Jumbles, one letter to
each square, to form words. Each word
will be represented in the picture on the
previous page.

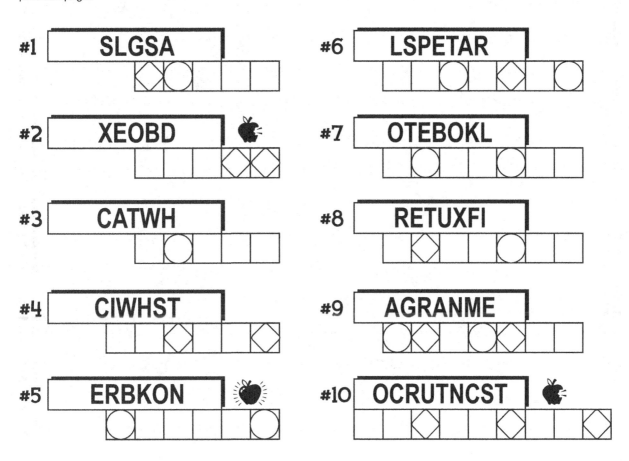

#1 SLGSA

#2 XEOBD

#3 CATWH

#4 CIWHST

#5 ERBKON

#6 LSPETAR

#7 OTEBOKL

#8 RETUXFI

#9 AGRANME

#10 OCRUTNCST

Arrange the circled letters to solve mystery answer #1. Arrange the diamonded letters to solve mystery
answer #2. Clues to the mystery answers can be found somewhere in the picture on the previous page.

CLUE #1 Making instruction books can be considered this.
MYSTERY
ANSWER #1

CLUE #2 Checking the lamp instruction book was this.
MYSTERY
ANSWER #2

EVERY ANSWER HAS
SOMETHING TO DO WITH
THE JUMBLE PICTURE.

Two-in-One JUMBLE
SEE&SEARCH™

Unscramble the Jumbles, one letter to
each square, to form words. Each word
will be represented in the picture on the
previous page.

#1 ELONR

#2 HCUCO

#3 LGMIEN

#4 LUSEOB

#5 YTATHC

#6 IKNPAN

#7 CTATKA

#8 TUBNTO

#9 AESDHET

#10 RDKAECC

Arrange the circled letters to solve mystery answer #1. Arrange the diamonded letters to solve mystery
answer #2. Clues to the mystery answers can be found somewhere in the picture on the previous page.

CLUE #1   What the telemarketer considered her job to be.
MYSTERY
ANSWER #1   A ⬭⬭⬭⬭⬭⬭⬭

CLUE #2   What the telemarketer made at the party.
MYSTERY
ANSWER #2   A ◇◇◇◇◇◇◇◇◇◇◇

79

EVERY ANSWER HAS
SOMETHING TO DO WITH
THE JUMBLE PICTURE.

Two-in-One **JUMBLE**
SEE&SEARCH ™

Unscramble the Jumbles, one letter to
each square, to form words. Each word
will be represented in the picture on the
previous page.

#1 OHOD

#2 RHSTA

#3 PERAP

#4 ODARI

#5 EUNTNL

#6 KARTSC

#7 RIZLAD

#8 AOESOBC

#9 MECMUTO

#10 AGRNINW

#11 TNSTOAI

Arrange the circled letters to solve mystery answer #1. Arrange the diamonded letters to solve mystery
answer #2. Clues to the mystery answers can be found somewhere in the picture on the previous page.

CLUE #1   The forgetful businessman lost this.

MYSTERY
ANSWER #1   HIS ⬡⬡⬡⬡⬡ OF ⬡⬡⬡⬡⬡⬡⬡

CLUE #2   This is how the lifeguard got to work.

MYSTERY
ANSWER #2   A ⬚⬚⬚⬚ ⬚⬚⬚⬚

JUMBLE SEE&SEARCH™

Three-in-One

LOTS OF JUMBLES®
THREE DIFFERENT MYSTERY ANSWERS
EVERY ANSWER HAS SOMETHING
TO DO WITH THE PICTURE

We've put a lot of Jumbles® in each puzzle and put three different Jumble® mystery answers into the same picture. Can you find all the Jumbles® in the picture? Can you figure out which parts of the picture will help you solve the mystery answers?

Unscramble the mixed up letters to make words. If you get stumped, look at the picture. Each and every answer has something to do with the picture ... all you have to do is find it. Some Jumbles® are verbs and are shown with the symbol 🍎. Other Jumbles® are adjectives and are shown with this symbol: 🍎.

You'll be solving THREE different Jumble® mystery answers in the "THREE-IN-ONE" puzzles. You'll have to look at the picture for help. Each mystery answer will correspond to one part of the picture.

"THREE-IN-ONE" Jumble® See & Search™ is three times the fun.

EVERY ANSWER HAS SOMETHING TO DO WITH THE PICTURE

JUMBLE. SEE&SEARCH™

Three-in-One

#1 EHBCN

#2 ILTPU

CLUE #1 What emerged when the wind blew off his toupee.

MYSTERY ANSWER #1 THE ⬡⬡⬡⬡ ⬡⬡⬡⬡⬡

JUMBLE SEE&SEARCH #42

I think you're missing something.

Right on time

Where did you get that watch?

That's just a typo.

I've never heard of a Rolatimex.

EVERY ANSWER HAS SOMETHING TO DO WITH THE JUMBLE PICTURE. **Three-in-One** **JUMBLE. SEE&SEARCH™**

Unscramble the Jumbles, one letter to each square, to form words. Each word will be represented in the picture on the previous page.

#1 EHBCN

#2 ILTPU

#3 SINSWG

#4 GROEJG

#5 OEGNIP

#6 LGELNSI

#7 TESUDHL

#8 CPKKBACA

#9 ATNUIOFN

#10 URBEYSLT

Arrange the circled letters to solve mystery answer #1. Arrange the diamonded letters to solve mystery answer #2. Arrange the clouded letters to solve mystery answer #3. Clues to the mystery answers can be found somewhere in the picture on the previous page.

THREE MYSTERY ANSWERS

CLUE #1 What emerged when the wind blew off his toupee.

MYSTERY ANSWER #1 THE ⬡⬡⬡⬡ ⬡⬡⬡⬡⬡

CLUE #2 The preacher exercised this way.

MYSTERY ANSWER #2 ◇◇◇◇◇◇◇◇◇◇◇◇◇

CLUE #3 Good advice when offered a time piece on the street.

MYSTERY ANSWER #3 ☁☁☁☁☁ ☁☁☁

83

Unscramble the Jumbles, one letter to
each square, to form words. Each word
will be represented in the picture on the
previous page.

#1 **OEYNM**

#6 **TWEOBI**

#2 **YGANR**

#7 **IFAPRECI**

#3 **LERTAT**

#8 **ILOBDLFL**

#4 **ESPUSR**

#9 **GGRAHCNI**

#5 **EFDTTI**

#10 **RCETSALOA**

Arrange the circled letters to solve mystery answer #1. Arrange the diamonded letters to solve mystery
answer #2. Arrange the clouded letters to solve mystery answer #3. Clues to the mystery answers can
be found somewhere in the picture on the previous page.

CLUE #1 A purse sale can cause this.

MYSTERY
ANSWER #1 A ⬡⬡⬡⬡ ⬡⬡⬡

CLUE #2 Often harder than a diamond.

MYSTERY
ANSWER #2

CLUE #3 His wife thought this about his new outfit.

MYSTERY
ANSWER #3 IT

Three-in-One **JUMBLE** SEE&SEARCH™

Unscramble the Jumbles, one letter to
each square, to form words. Each word
will be represented in the picture on the
previous page.

#1 **RADST**

#6 **CADGNNI**

#2 **TMEYP**

#7 **KYWIESH**

#3 **ITUFR**

#8 **EPLISDL**

#4 **TOAOTT**

#9 **RCPNOOP**

#5 **EEMTHL**

#10 **ETACBELR**

Arrange the circled letters to solve mystery answer #1. Arrange the diamonded letters to solve mystery
answer #2. Arrange the clouded letters to solve mystery answer #3. Clues to the mystery answers can
be found somewhere in the picture on the previous page.

CLUE #1 This is a cure for dandruff.

MYSTERY
ANSWER #1

CLUE #2 Some people think a pub is good for this.

MYSTERY
ANSWER #2

CLUE #3 Even when he relaxed, the guitarist did this.

MYSTERY
ANSWER #3

EVERY ANSWER HAS
SOMETHING TO DO WITH
THE JUMBLE® PICTURE.

Three-in-One JUMBLE.
SEE & SEARCH ™

Unscramble the Jumbles, one letter to
each square, to form words. Each word
will be represented in the picture on the
previous page.

#1 EHBCN

#2 ILTPU

#3 SINSWG

#4 GROEJG

#5 OEGNIP

#6 LGELNSI

#7 TESUDHL

#8 CPKKBACA

#9 ATNUIOFN

#10 URBEYSLT

Arrange the circled letters to solve mystery answer #1. Arrange the diamonded letters to solve mystery
answer #2. Arrange the clouded letters to solve mystery answer #3. Clues to the mystery answers can
be found somewhere in the picture on the previous page.

CLUE #1 What emerged when the wind blew off his toupee.
MYSTERY
ANSWER #1 THE ◯◯◯◯ ◯◯◯◯◯

CLUE #2 The preacher exercised this way.
MYSTERY
ANSWER #2 ◇◇◇◇◇◇◇◇◇◇◇◇

CLUE #3 Good advice when offered a timepiece on the street.
MYSTERY
ANSWER #3 ☁☁☁☁☁ ☁☁☁

89

Three-in-One JUMBLE®
SEE&SEARCH™

Unscramble the Jumbles, one letter to
each square, to form words. Each word
will be represented in the picture on the
previous page.

#1 VYWA

#2 NOEHP

#3 PSMUT

#4 RACON

#5 DRERUD

#6 KETACL

#7 EBBWCO

#8 DLAIGNN

#9 IGWHOLN

#10 SRIURQEL

Arrange the circled letters to solve mystery answer #1. Arrange the diamonded letters to solve mystery
answer #2. Arrange the clouded letters to solve mystery answer #3. Clues to the mystery answers can
be found somewhere in the picture on the previous page.

CLUE #1 Word that they're biting can do this to a busy executive.

MYSTERY ANSWER #1 ⬡⭕⭕⭕⭕ HIM ⭕⭕⭕⭕

CLUE #2 What the novice fisherman ended up with.

MYSTERY ANSWER #2 A ◇◇◇◇ ◇◇◇◇◇◇◇

CLUE #3 What the comedian duck was good at.

MYSTERY ANSWER #3 ☁☁☁☁ ☁☁☁☁☁

91

Three-in-One JUMBLE® SEE&SEARCH™

Unscramble the Jumbles, one letter to
each square, to form words. Each word
will be represented in the picture on the
previous page.

#1 KEDC

#2 EAWRG

#3 DALHEN

#4 ODLARL

#5 BRESMUN

#6 ENROBUC

#7 KPATJCO

#8 RESCUYIT

#9 PNSINRSE

#10 NBLAMGGI

Arrange the circled letters to solve mystery answer #1. Arrange the diamonded letters to solve mystery
answer #2. Arrange the clouded letters to solve mystery answer #3. Clues to the mystery answers can
be found somewhere in the picture on the previous page.

CLUE #1 A night at the casino can be this.
MYSTERY
ANSWER #1

CLUE #2 What getting dealt four of a kind is.
MYSTERY
ANSWER #2 A

CLUE #3 Why she tried the cigar.
MYSTERY
ANSWER #3 FOR A

93

EVERY ANSWER HAS
SOMETHING TO DO WITH
THE JUMBLE® PICTURE.

JUMBLE.
SEE & SEARCH™

Unscramble the Jumbles, one letter to
each square, to form words. Each word
will be represented in the picture on the
previous page.

#1 GLAEE

#2 OTVID

#3 TARWE

#4 SNORI

#5 DIRBEI

#6 WGSNIS

#7 EMDANGL

#8 TANADHRC

#9 TCARPCIE

#10 SLOBECUHU

Arrange the circled letters to solve mystery answer #1. Arrange the diamonded letters to solve mystery
answer #2. Arrange the clouded letters to solve mystery answer #3. Clues to the mystery answers can
be found somewhere in the picture on the previous page.

CLUE #1 What it takes to be a winning golfer.

MYSTERY
ANSWER #1 A ◯◯◯ OF ◯◯◯◯◯

CLUE #2 What balding jokes do after a while.

MYSTERY
ANSWER #2 ◇◇◇◇◇ ◇◇◇◇◇

CLUE #3 The golfer had to change socks because he had this.

MYSTERY
ANSWER #3 A ▢▢▢▢ IN ▢▢▢

95

Unscramble the Jumbles, one letter to
each square, to form words. Each word
will be represented in the picture on the
previous page.

#1 DEWSE

#6 TINAILI

#2 LERBID

#7 RUTEVLU

#3 UGNOTE

#8 GICNFNE

#4 LEDADSD

#9 CRAHPAOP

#5 NVIOSEB

#10 TFLUTRBYE

Arrange the circled letters to solve mystery answer #1. Arrange the diamonded letters to solve mystery
answer #2. Arrange the clouded letters to solve mystery answer #3. Clues to the mystery answers can
be found somewhere in the picture on the previous page.

CLUE #1 The pony had trouble speaking because he was this.

MYSTERY
ANSWER #1 A ◯◯◯◯◯◯ ◯◯◯◯◯

CLUE #2 Where the farmer went when he retired.

MYSTERY
ANSWER #2 ◇◇◇ TO ◇◇◇◇◇◇◇

CLUE #3 The cow lying around was this.

MYSTERY
ANSWER #3 ☁☁☁☁☁☁ ☁☁☁

Three-in-One **JUMBLE** SEE&SEARCH™

Unscramble the Jumbles, one letter to
each square, to form words. Each word
will be represented in the picture on the
previous page.

#1 GIYPG

#2 RYTID

#3 DEFLIS

#4 KECBTU

#5 UYBHBC

#6 ORCATTR

#7 TROFOPO

#8 ATLENTF

#9 IGAGGNW

#10 UNAGLIGH

Arrange the circled letters to solve mystery answer #1. Arrange the diamonded letters to solve mystery
answer #2. Arrange the clouded letters to solve mystery answer #3. Clues to the mystery answers can
be found somewhere in the picture on the previous page.

CLUE #1 The successful pig farmer was this.

MYSTERY
ANSWER #1

CLUE #2 The spider that lived in the corn made one.

MYSTERY
ANSWER #2 A

CLUE #3 The animals thought the farmer's jokes were this.

MYSTERY
ANSWER #3

Three-in-One  JUMBLE®
SEE&SEARCH™

Unscramble the Jumbles, one letter to
each square, to form words. Each word
will be represented in the picture on the
previous page.

#1 PDIR

#2 ROWM

#3 KUCTR

#4 SIDYA

#5 CRBHAN

#6 RBEARL

#7 EBVARE

#8 LWHOLO

#9 NGIGIGD

#10 RELSURQI

Arrange the circled letters to solve mystery answer #1. Arrange the diamonded letters to solve mystery
answer #2. Arrange the clouded letters to solve mystery answer #3. Clues to the mystery answers can
be found somewhere in the picture on the previous page.

CLUE #1 The gardener feels this way at the end of the day.

MYSTERY
ANSWER #1

CLUE #2 The tree doctor got to this.

MYSTERY
ANSWER #2 THE ☐☐☐☐ OF THE ☐☐☐☐☐☐☐

CLUE #3 The type of romance had by gardeners.

MYSTERY
ANSWER #3

EVERY ANSWER HAS
SOMETHING TO DO WITH
THE JUMBLE® PICTURE.

Three-in-One

Unscramble the Jumbles, one letter to
each square, to form words. Each word
will be represented in the picture on the
previous page.

#1 SMBIL

#2 KSNUK

#3 SOWOD

#4 DILBN

#5 OPTEIT

#6 RIDFAA

#7 LZYRGIZ

#8 LTHESWI

#9 NUCPKHIM

#10 OLKAPBOY

Arrange the circled letters to solve mystery answer #1. Arrange the diamonded letters to solve mystery
answer #2. Arrange the clouded letters to solve mystery answer #3. Clues to the mystery answers can
be found somewhere in the picture on the previous page.

CLUE #1 What the timid hunter did.
MYSTERY
ANSWER #1 ⬡⬡⬡⬡⬡⬡ THE ⬡⬡⬡⬡

CLUE #2 The coach followed one on his hunting trip.
MYSTERY
ANSWER #2 A ⬡⬡⬡⬡ ⬡⬡⬡⬡

CLUE #3 Not seeing any ducks left the hunters feeling this way.
MYSTERY
ANSWER #3 IN A ⬡⬡⬡⬡ ⬡⬡⬡⬡

103

Three-in-One JUMBLE®
SEE&SEARCH™

Unscramble the Jumbles, one letter to
each square, to form words. Each word
will be represented in the picture on the
previous page.

#1 ATLNP

#2 OLVINI

#3 SEHECE

#4 IGTADN

#5 ONKDROBO

#6 CRETNANE

#7 SRECKRAC

#8 ALITFEBUU

#9 RUSTMIDKC

#10 SLISFELHH

Arrange the circled letters to solve mystery answer #1. Arrange the diamonded letters to solve mystery
answer #2. Arrange the clouded letters to solve mystery answer #3. Clues to the mystery answers can
be found somewhere in the picture on the previous page.

CLUE #1   The model ate off of _____ plates.
MYSTERY
ANSWER #1

CLUE #2   A corkscrew might also be useful for opening this.
MYSTERY
ANSWER #2   A

CLUE #3   What the gossip turned an earful into.
MYSTERY
ANSWER #3   A

Three-in-One

Unscramble the Jumbles, one letter to
each square, to form words. Each word
will be represented in the picture on the
previous page.

#1 **LKULS**

#2 **GAERV**

#3 **TIHWC**

#4 **KOPOSS**

#5 **ARPIET**

#6 **UDANTHE**

#7 **URTVELU**

#8 **KIMPUNP**

#9 **IDIEMCNE**

#10 **OPSOTERD**

Arrange the circled letters to solve mystery answer #1. Arrange the diamonded letters to solve mystery
answer #2. Arrange the clouded letters to solve mystery answer #3. Clues to the mystery answers can
be found somewhere in the picture on the previous page.

CLUE #1 The ghost lived on one.

MYSTERY
ANSWER #1 **A** ☐☐☐☐ ☐☐☐

CLUE #2 What the ghost considered his new girlfriend to be.

MYSTERY
ANSWER #2 **A** ☐☐☐☐ ☐☐☐☐

CLUE #3 What the doctor's son made on Halloween.

MYSTERY
ANSWER #3 ☐☐☐☐☐ ☐☐☐☐

EVERY ANSWER HAS
SOMETHING TO DO WITH
THE JUMBLE® PICTURE.

Unscramble the Jumbles, one letter to
each square, to form words. Each word
will be represented in the picture on the
previous page.

#1 TOLEBT

#2 PNDAME

#3 ROCNAH

#4 GLEUNO

#5 GEREBIC

#6 SPOOTCU

#7 NEGIUPN

#8 CLEEKANC

#9 DREASTDN

#10 EBLFIOAT

Arrange the circled letters to solve mystery answer #1. Arrange the diamonded letters to solve mystery
answer #2. Arrange the clouded letters to solve mystery answer #3. Clues to the mystery answers can
be found somewhere in the picture on the previous page.

CLUE #1 What she hoped to find on her vacation ship.

MYSTERY
ANSWER #1 A ◯◯◯◯◯◯◯◯◯◯

CLUE #2 What the captain of the vacation ship had.

MYSTERY
ANSWER #2

CLUE #3 How the finely dressed passenger looked on the ship.

MYSTERY
ANSWER #3

109

EVERY ANSWER HAS
SOMETHING TO DO WITH
THE JUMBLE® PICTURE.

Three-in-One

JUMBLE®
SEE&SEARCH™

Unscramble the Jumbles, one letter to
each square, to form words. Each word
will be represented in the picture on the
previous page.

#1 SGSLA

#6 HRAHTAD

#2 ROLTWE

#7 DCATIECN

#3 NDOWIW

#8 IBTAONMI

#4 EVLHOS

#9 CTNSOTCRU

#5 GETFAUI

#10 REPTUBLIN

Arrange the circled letters to solve mystery answer #1. Arrange the diamonded letters to solve mystery
answer #2. Arrange the clouded letters to solve mystery answer #3. Clues to the mystery answers can
be found somewhere in the picture on the previous page.

CLUE #1   A brick layer's ailment.

MYSTERY
ANSWER #1

CLUE #2   What the cement tycoon sought.

MYSTERY
ANSWER #2

CLUE #3   What the ambitious architect had.

MYSTERY
ANSWER #3

JUMBLE® SEE&SEARCH™

Busy, Busy, Busy

LOTS OF JUMBLES®
LOTS GOING ON
EVERY ANSWER HAS SOMETHING
TO DO WITH THE PICTURE

We've put a lot of Jumbles® in each puzzle and created a very busy scene in the pictures. Can you find all the Jumbles® in the picture? Can you figure out which parts of the picture will help you solve the mystery answers?

Unscramble the mixed up letters to make words. If you get stumped, look at the picture. Each and every answer has something to do with the picture ... all you have to do is find it. Some Jumbles® are verbs and are shown with the symbol 🍎 . Other Jumbles® are adjectives and are shown with this symbol: 💥 .

You'll be solving two different Jumble® mystery answers in the "BUSY, BUSY, BUSY" puzzles. You'll have to look at the picture for help. Each mystery answer will correspond to one part of the picture.

Get busy ...

EVERY ANSWER HAS SOMETHING TO DO WITH THE PICTURE

JUMBLE® SEE&SEARCH™

Busy, Busy, Busy

#1 **LORTL**

CLUE #1 There is this kind of plant in the picture.
MYSTERY ANSWER #1 A ☐☐☐☐☐ OF ☐☐☐☐☐☐☐

JUMBLE SEE&SEARCH #59

JQ2A3

He's bluffing!

EVERY ANSWER HAS SOMETHING TO DO WITH THE JUMBLE PICTURE.

Busy, Busy, Busy

JUMBLE® SEE&SEARCH™

Unscramble the Jumbles, one letter to each square, to form words. Each word will be represented in the picture on the previous page.

#1 **LORTL**

#2 **YIAFR**

#3 **ENUEQ**

#4 **GOMNE**

#5 **GONRAD**

#6 **THINKG**

#7 **CNABLYO**

#8 **WABNIRO**

#9 **RUNINCO**

#10 **ACLIMGA**

#11 **STAYNAF**

#12 **SOMOHURM**

Arrange the circled letters to solve mystery answer #1. Arrange the diamonded letters to solve mystery answer #2. Clues to the mystery answers can be found somewhere in the picture on the previous page.

CLUE #1 There is this kind of plant in the picture.
MYSTERY ANSWER #1 A ☐☐☐☐☐ OF ☐☐☐☐☐☐☐

CLUE #2 You can see this place in the picture.
MYSTERY ANSWER #2 A ☐☐☐☐☐☐ ☐☐☐☐☐☐☐☐

113

Unscramble the Jumbles, one letter to
each square, to form words. Each word
will be represented in the picture on the
previous page.

#1 ERIZP

#7 TACRSOE

#2 NLWOC

#8 ANCLPIE

#3 SFYIHT

#9 SINTSOG

#4 EKTCIT

#10 NLIVCRAA

#5 WIMDYA

#11 LSEALBAB

#6 LOLAONB

Arrange the circled letters to solve mystery answer #1. Arrange the diamonded letters to solve mystery
answer #2. Clues to the mystery answers can be found somewhere in the picture on the previous page.

CLUE #1 _____ _____ can be seen in this picture.
MYSTERY
ANSWER #1

CLUE #2 This was introduced in 1893 in Chicago.
MYSTERY
ANSWER #2 THE

Busy,
Busy,
Busy

JUMBLE®
SEE & SEARCH ™

Unscramble the Jumbles, one letter to
each square, to form words. Each word
will be represented in the picture on the
previous page.

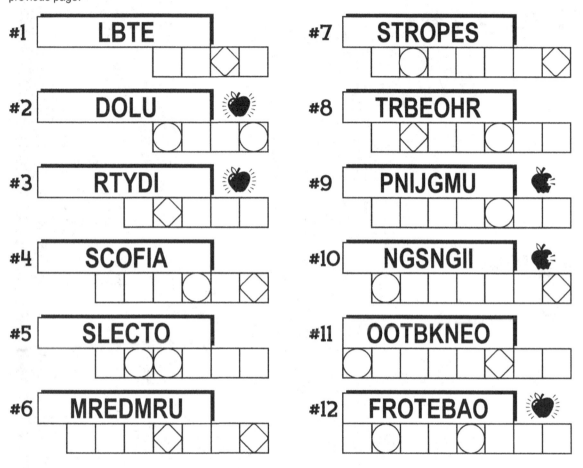

#1 LBTE

#2 DOLU

#3 RTYDI

#4 SCOFIA

#5 SLECTO

#6 MREDMRU

#7 STROPES

#8 TRBEOHR

#9 PNIJGMU

#10 NGSNGII

#11 OOTBKNEO

#12 FROTEBAO

Arrange the circled letters to solve mystery answer #1. Arrange the diamonded letters to solve mystery
answer #2. Clues to the mystery answers can be found somewhere in the picture on the previous page.

CLUE #1 Three of these can be seen in this picture.

MYSTERY
ANSWER #1

CLUE #2 This can be seen in the picture.

MYSTERY
ANSWER #2 A

EVERY ANSWER HAS SOMETHING TO DO WITH THE JUMBLE® PICTURE.

Unscramble the Jumbles, one letter to each square, to form words. Each word will be represented in the picture on the previous page.

#1 **OCTAR**

#2 **HUSRE**

#3 **ASBEM**

#4 **ODRWC**

#5 **IVSEMO**

#6 **RAPCTE**

#7 **IERPMRE**

#8 **PREPHOC**

#9 **RAACESM**

#10 **OLONLABS**

#11 **UEFACFHUR**

#12 **ROGPTAAUH**

Arrange the circled letters to solve mystery answer #1. Arrange the diamonded letters to solve mystery answer #2. Clues to the mystery answers can be found somewhere in the picture on the previous page.

CLUE #1 There are three of these in the picture.

MYSTERY ANSWER #1

CLUE #2 There is one of these in the picture.

MYSTERY ANSWER #2

119

Unscramble the Jumbles, one letter to
each square, to form words. Each word
will be represented in the picture on the
previous page.

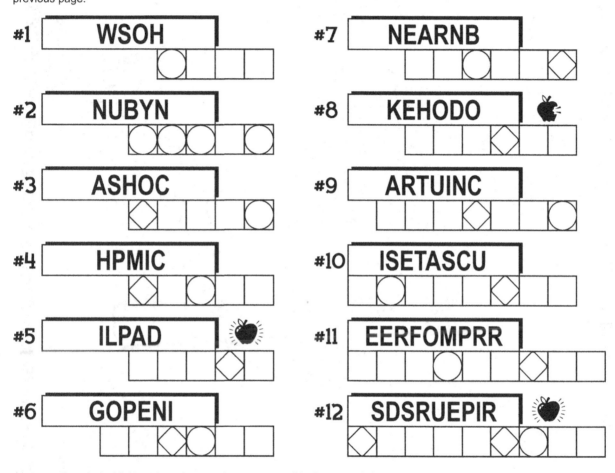

#1 WSOH

#2 NUBYN

#3 ASHOC

#4 HPMIC

#5 ILPAD

#6 GOPENI

#7 NEARNB

#8 KEHODO

#9 ARTUINC

#10 ISETASCU

#11 EERFOMPRR

#12 SDSRUEPIR

Arrange the circled letters to solve mystery answer #1. Arrange the diamonded letters to solve mystery
answer #2. Clues to the mystery answers can be found somewhere in the picture on the previous page.

CLUE #1 This is what the comic/magician considered his job to be.

MYSTERY
ANSWER #1

CLUE #2 There are several of these in the picture.

MYSTERY
ANSWER #2

EVERY ANSWER HAS
SOMETHING TO DO WITH
THE JUMBLE® PICTURE.

JUMBLE.
SEE & SEARCH ™

Unscramble the Jumbles, one letter to
each square, to form words. Each word
will be represented in the picture on the
previous page.

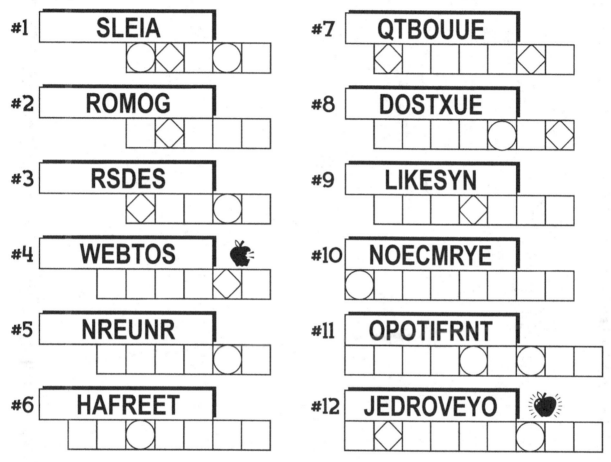

#1 SLEIA

#2 ROMOG

#3 RSDES

#4 WEBTOS

#5 NREUNR

#6 HAFREET

#7 QTBOUUE

#8 DOSTXUE

#9 LIKESYN

#10 NOECMRYE

#11 OPOTIFRNT

#12 JEDROVEYO

Arrange the circled letters to solve mystery answer #1. Arrange the diamonded letters to solve mystery
answer #2. Clues to the mystery answers can be found somewhere in the picture on the previous page.

CLUE #1   You can see this in the picture.
MYSTERY
ANSWER #1   A ◯◯◯◯◯◯◯   ◯◯◯

CLUE #2   You can see a pair of these in the picture.
MYSTERY
ANSWER #2   ◇◇◇◇◇   ◇◇◇◇◇

Unscramble the Jumbles, one letter to
each square, to form words. Each word
will be represented in the picture on the
previous page.

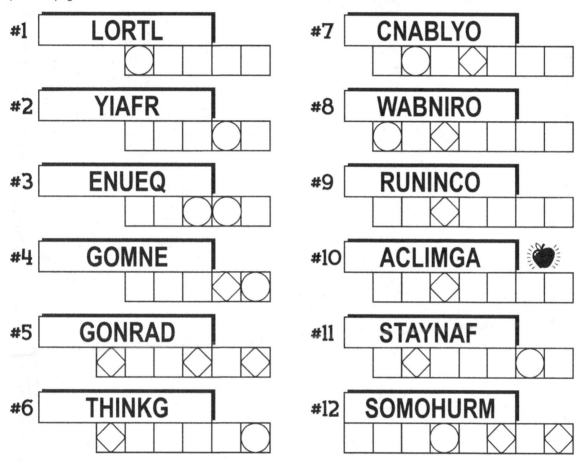

#1 LORTL

#2 YIAFR

#3 ENUEQ

#4 GOMNE

#5 GONRAD

#6 THINKG

#7 CNABLYO

#8 WABNIRO

#9 RUNINCO

#10 ACLIMGA

#11 STAYNAF

#12 SOMOHURM

Arrange the circled letters to solve mystery answer #1. Arrange the diamonded letters to solve mystery
answer #2. Clues to the mystery answers can be found somewhere in the picture on the previous page.

CLUE #1 There is this kind of plant in the picture.

MYSTERY
ANSWER #1   A ⬭⬭⬭⬭⬭ OF ⬭⬭⬭⬭⬭⬭⬭

CLUE #2 You can see this place in the picture.

MYSTERY
ANSWER #2   A ◇◇◇◇◇◇ ◇◇◇◇◇◇◇◇

JUMBLE® SEE&SEARCH™

Busy, Busy, Busy

EVERY ANSWER HAS SOMETHING TO DO WITH THE JUMBLE® PICTURE.

Unscramble the Jumbles, one letter to each square, to form words. Each word will be represented in the picture on the previous page.

#1 PLAEP ⬜⬜⬜⭕⬜

#2 REEBT ⬜⭕⬜⬜⬜

#3 SVACNA ⬜⬜⭕⬜⬜⭕

#4 SRAERE ⭕⬜⬜⬜⬜⬜

#5 OUSTDI ⬜⬜⬜◇⬜⬜

#6 CHEKTS ⬜⬜◇⬜⬜⬜

#7 LTUCSP ⬜⬜⬜⬜◇⬜

#8 WOKMAH ⭕⬜⬜⬜⬜⬜

#9 CTBUJES ⬜⬜◇⬜⬜⬜⬜

#10 ALISDPY ⬜◇⬜⭕⬜⬜⬜

#11 TRIPNAE ⬜⭕⬜◇⬜⬜⬜

#12 ATROIRPT ⬜⭕⬜⬜⬜⬜⬜⬜

Arrange the circled letters to solve mystery answer #1. Arrange the diamonded letters to solve mystery answer #2. Clues to the mystery answers can be found somewhere in the picture on the previous page.

CLUE #1 You can find this in an art class.

MYSTERY ANSWER #1 ⭕⭕⭕⭕⭕ ⭕⭕⭕⭕

CLUE #2 There is one of these in the picture.

MYSTERY ANSWER #2 **AN** ◇◇◇◇◇

127

JUMBLE® SEE&SEARCH™

EVERY ANSWER HAS SOMETHING TO DO WITH THE JUMBLE® PICTURE.

Unscramble the Jumbles, one letter to each square, to form words. Each word will be represented in the picture on the previous page.

Busy, Busy, Busy

#1 LBMUA

#2 UMTSR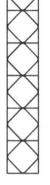

#3 RDCHO

#4 PLOTPA

#5 HMRTYH

#6 CLASOV

#7 SRCLYI

#8 LIFDED

#9 MYSLCAB

#10 ILAGTERN

#11 OAICHMNRA

#12 DRCROEGIN

Arrange the circled letters to solve mystery answer #1. Arrange the diamonded letters to solve mystery answer #2. Clues to the mystery answers can be found somewhere in the picture on the previous page.

CLUE #1   There are six of these in this picture.

MYSTERY ANSWER #1

CLUE #2   There is one of these in this picture.

MYSTERY ANSWER #2   A

129

130

JUMBLE® SEE&SEARCH™

Busy, Busy, Busy

EVERY ANSWER HAS SOMETHING TO DO WITH THE JUMBLE® PICTURE.

Unscramble the Jumbles, one letter to each square, to form words. Each word will be represented in the picture on the previous page.

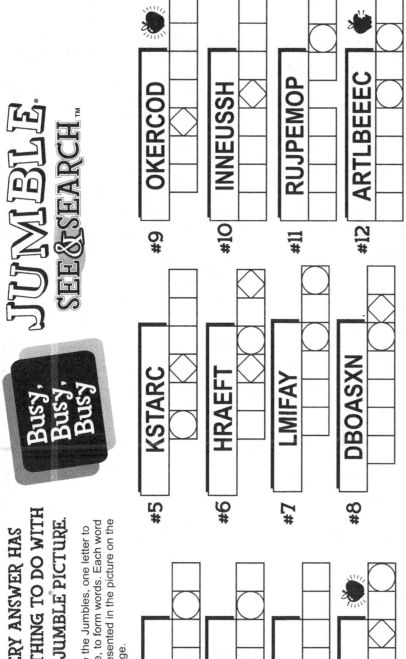

#1 DAPAN

#2 TIKRS

#3 IFSGT

#4 PYAPH

#5 KSTARC

#6 HRAEFT

#7 LMIFAY

#8 DBOASXN

#9 OKERCOD

#10 INNEUSSH

#11 RUJPEMOP

#12 ARTLBEEC

Arrange the circled letters to solve mystery answer #1. Arrange the diamonded letters to solve mystery answer #2. Clues to the mystery answers can be found somewhere in the picture on the previous page.

CLUE #1   There is one of these in the picture.

MYSTERY ANSWER #1   A ⬡⬡⬡⬡⬡⬡⬡

CLUE #2   There is one of these in this picture.

MYSTERY ANSWER #2   A ◇◇◇◇◇◇◇◇◇◇

131

JUMBLE SEE&SEARCH™

EVERY ANSWER HAS SOMETHING TO DO WITH THE JUMBLE PICTURE.

Unscramble the Jumbles, one letter to each square, to form words. Each word will be represented in the picture on the previous page.

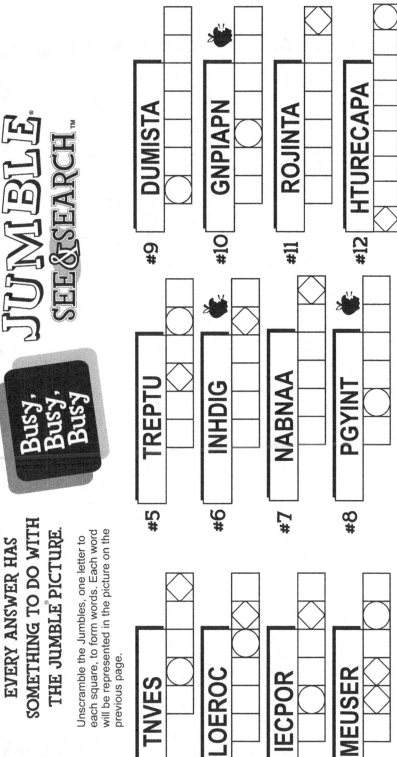

Busy, Busy, Busy

#1 TNVES

#2 LOEROC

#3 IECPOR

#4 MEUSER

#5 TREPTU

#6 INHDIG

#7 NABNAA

#8 PGYINT

#9 DUMISTA

#10 GNPIAPN

#11 ROJINTA

#12 HTURECAPA

Arrange the circled letters to solve mystery answer #1. Arrange the diamonded letters to solve mystery answer #2. Clues to the mystery answers can be found somewhere in the picture on the previous page.

CLUE #1 There are eight of these in the picture.

MYSTERY ANSWER #1 ○○○○○○○

CLUE #2 This does not belong in the picture.

MYSTERY ANSWER #2 A ◇◇◇◇◇◇◇

133

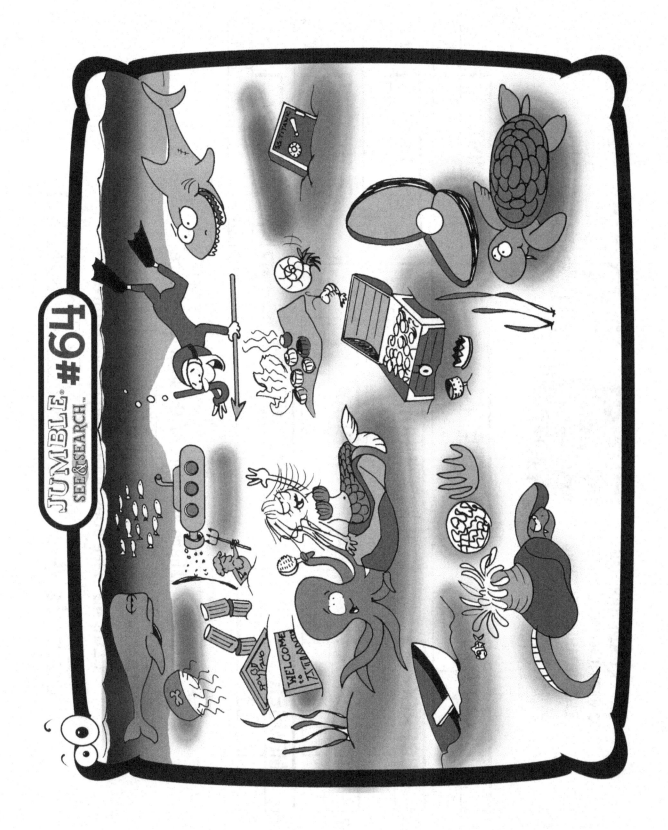

134

JUMBLE® SEE & SEARCH™

EVERY ANSWER HAS SOMETHING TO DO WITH THE JUMBLE® PICTURE.

Unscramble the Jumbles, one letter to each square, to form words. Each word will be represented in the picture on the previous page.

Busy, Busy, Busy

#1 NIRUS

#2 VNIGWA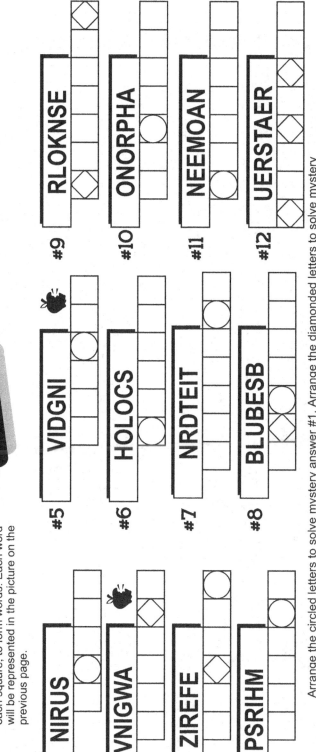

#3 ZIREFE

#4 PSRIHM

#5 VIDGNI

#6 HOLOCS

#7 NRDTEIT

#8 BLUBESB

#9 RLOKNSE

#10 ONORPHA

#11 NEEMOAN

#12 UERSTAER

Arrange the circled letters to solve mystery answer #1. Arrange the diamonded letters to solve mystery answer #2. Clues to the mystery answers can be found somewhere in the picture on the previous page.

CLUE #1   There is a _____ in the picture.

MYSTERY ANSWER #1

CLUE #2   There is one of these swimming in the picture.

MYSTERY ANSWER #2   A

135

JUMBLE® SEE&SEARCH™

EVERY ANSWER HAS SOMETHING TO DO WITH THE JUMBLE® PICTURE.

Unscramble the Jumbles, one letter to each square, to form words. Each word will be represented in the picture on the previous page.

Busy, Busy, Busy

#1 BATU

#2 LWPO

#3 TKTIY

#4 CBNEH

#5 OKCLC

#6 KEYHCO

#7 EVSOLH

#8 HANYRTD

#9 DEAGNIR

#10 SREQILUR

#11 LBSALOWN

#12 ANPILEAR

Arrange the circled letters to solve mystery answer #1. Arrange the diamonded letters to solve mystery answer #2. Clues to the mystery answers can be found somewhere in the picture on the previous page.

CLUE #1   There are a few different _____ that can be seen in this picture.

MYSTERY ANSWER #1   ⭕⭕⭕⭕⭕⭕⭕

CLUE #2   A _____ can be seen in this picture.

MYSTERY ANSWER #2   ◇◇◇ ◇◇◇◇◇

137

JUMBLE. SEE&SEARCH™

Photo Jumble®

LOTS OF JUMBLES®
LOTS GOING ON
EVERY ANSWER HAS SOMETHING
TO DO WITH THE PHOTO

We've put a lot of Jumbles in each puzzle and created a very busy scene in the photo. Can you find all the Jumbles® in the photo? Can you figure out which parts of the photo will help you solve the mystery answers?

Unscramble the mixed up letters to make words. If you get stumped, look at the picture. Each and every answer has something to do with the picture ... all you have to do is find it.

You'll be solving one Jumble® mystery answer in the "PHOTO JUMBLE" puzzles. You'll have to look at the picture for help. The answer will correspond to one part of the photo.

EVERY ANSWER HAS SOMETHING TO DO WITH THE PICTURE

JUMBLE® SEE&SEARCH™

Photo Jumble®

#1 KMSA

CLUE   There is a _____ _____ in this picture.

MYSTERY ANSWER

JUMBLE SEE&SEARCH #69

EVERY ANSWER HAS SOMETHING TO DO WITH THE JUMBLE PICTURE.

Unscramble the Jumbles, one letter to each square, to form words. Each word will be represented in the picture on the previous page.

#1 KMSA

#2 UELFT

#3 VOELG

#4 RAGUTI

#5 TOLEUT

#6 UERQATC

#7 GSTRNIS

#8 ODRABYEK

#9 STACTESE

#10 NOBGREMOA

Arrange the circled letters to solve the mystery answer. Clues to the mystery answer can be found somewhere in the picture on the previous page.

CLUE   There is a _____ _____ in this picture.

MYSTERY ANSWER

Photography provided by KingenSmith Productions, Chicago, Illinois.

139

JUMBLE® SEE&SEARCH™

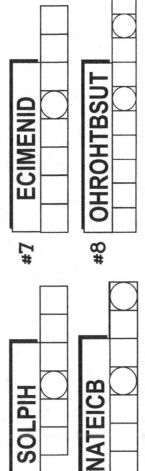

Photo Jumble®

EVERY ANSWER HAS SOMETHING TO DO WITH THE JUMBLE® PICTURE.

Unscramble the Jumbles, one letter to each square, to form words. Each word will be represented in the picture on the previous page.

#1 POAS

#2 LEOWT

#3 ZOARR

#4 SOLPIH

#5 NATEICB

#6 GLREPUN

#7 ECIMENID

#8 OHROHTBSUT

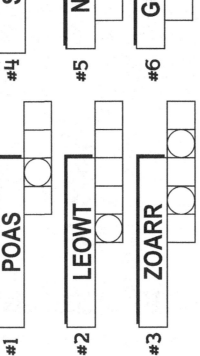

Arrange the circled letters to solve the mystery answer. Clues to the mystery answer can be found somewhere in the picture on the previous page.

CLUE   There are _____ in this picture.

MYSTERY ANSWER

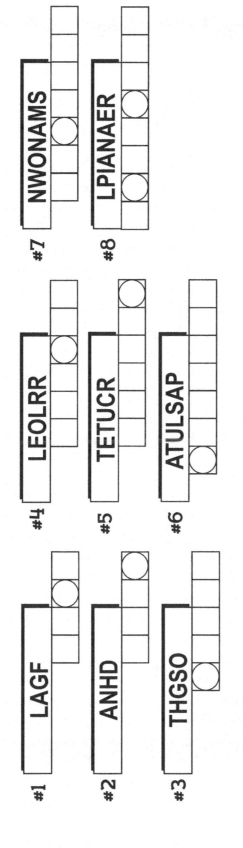

JUMBLE® SEE&SEARCH™

Photo Jumble®

EVERY ANSWER HAS SOMETHING TO DO WITH THE JUMBLE® PICTURE.

Unscramble the Jumbles, one letter to each square, to form words. Each word will be represented in the picture on the previous page.

#1 LAGF

#2 ANHD

#3 THGSO

#4 LEOLRR

#5 TETUCR

#6 ATULSAP

#7 NWONAMS

#8 LPIANAER

Arrange the circled letters to solve the mystery answer. Clues to the mystery answer can be found somewhere in the picture on the previous page.

CLUE   There is a _____ in this picture.

MYSTERY ANSWER

143

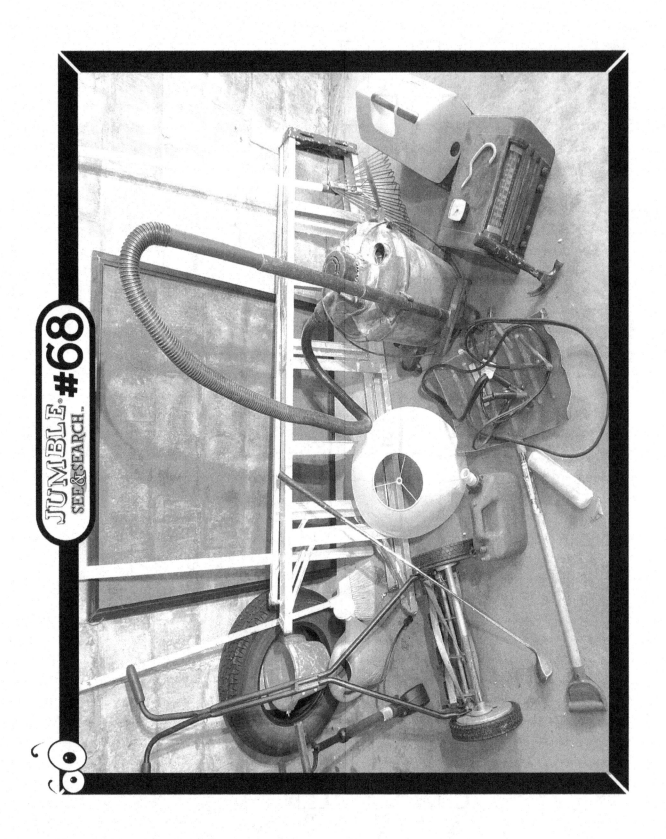

144

JUMBLE. SEE&SEARCH™

EVERY ANSWER HAS SOMETHING TO DO WITH THE JUMBLE PICTURE.

Unscramble the Jumbles, one letter to each square, to form words. Each word will be represented in the picture on the previous page.

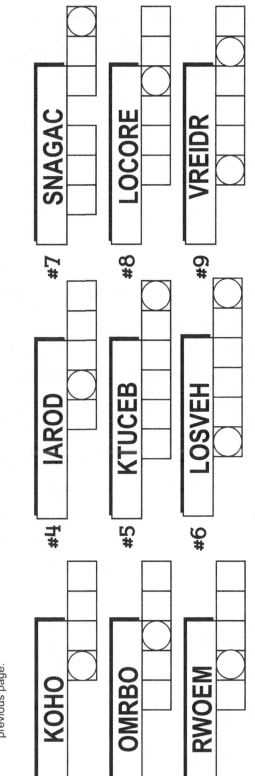

#1 KOHO

#2 OMRBO

#3 RWOEM

#4 IAROD

#5 KTUCEB

#6 LOSVEH

#7 SNAGAC

#8 LOCORE

#9 VREIDR

Arrange the circled letters to solve the mystery answer. Clues to the mystery answer can be found somewhere in the picture on the previous page.

CLUE   There are a lot of _____ in this picture.

MYSTERY ANSWER

EVERY ANSWER HAS
SOMETHING TO DO WITH
THE JUMBLE® PICTURE.

JUMBLE®
SEE&SEARCH™

Unscramble the Jumbles, one letter to
each square, to form words. Each word
will be represented in the picture on the
previous page.

#1 KMSA

#2 UELFT

#3 VOELG

#4 RAGUTI

#5 TOLEUT

#6 UERQATC

#7 GSTRNIS

#8 ODRABYEK

#9 STACTESE

#10 NOBGREMOA

Arrange the circled letters to solve the mystery answer. Clues to the mystery
answer can be found somewhere in the picture on the previous page.

CLUE   There is a _____ _____ in this picture.

MYSTERY
ANSWER

JUMBLE.
SEE & SEARCH™

What's Different?

LOTS OF JUMBLES®

A CHANGING SERIES OF PICTURES

ONE NEW OBJECT GETS ADDED PER
PICTURE TO THE SECOND,
THIRD, AND FOURTH PICTURES
IN EACH SERIES

EVERY ANSWER CAN BE
FOUND IN THE PICTURE

Each puzzle and picture is part of a series of four in which one
new object per picture is added to the second, third, and fourth
pictures. Can you spot it? If you can, it will make it easier for
you to solve the puzzle.

Unscramble the mixed up letters to make words. If you get
stumped, look at the picture. Each and every answer has something
to do with the pictures . . . all you have to do is find it. Some Jumbles®
are verbs and are shown with the symbol 🍎 . Other Jumbles® are
adjectives and are shown with this symbol: 🍎 .

JUMBLE®
SEE & SEARCH™
What's Different?

CAN YOU
SPOT THE
ADDED
OBJECT?

JUMBLE® SEE&SEARCH™

What's Different?

EVERY ANSWER HAS SOMETHING TO DO WITH THE JUMBLE® PICTURE.

Unscramble the Jumbles, one letter to each square, to form words. Each word will be represented in the picture on the previous page.

#1 OYVIR

#2 RTKOS

#3 EYHAN

#4 CUPOH

#5 MALEC

#6 TABITHA

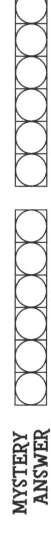

#7 PHINGOP

#8 SKESIWHR

Arrange the circled letters to solve the mystery answer. Clues to the mystery answer can be found somewhere in the picture on the previous page.

CLUE A favorite snack at the zoo.

MYSTERY ANSWER

JUMBLE® #71
SEE&SEARCH™

JUMBLE® SEE&SEARCH™

EVERY ANSWER HAS SOMETHING TO DO WITH THE JUMBLE® PICTURE.

What's Different?

Unscramble the Jumbles, one letter to each square, to form words. Each word will be represented in the picture on the previous page.

#1 YOJE

#2 ALOKA

#3 MLALA

#4 SOEOM

#5 FIPFUN

#6 PROHGE

#7 LEEGAB

#8 RLTOLERS

Arrange the circled letters to solve the mystery answer. Clues to the mystery answer can be found somewhere in the picture on the previous page.

CLUE Three _____ birds can be seen in this picture.

MYSTERY ANSWER

Arrange the diamonded letters to solve the mystery object. This object appears in the picture on the previous page but not in the previous picture(s) in the series.

Object that's been added to this picture

153

JUMBLE® SEE&SEARCH™

What's Different?

EVERY ANSWER HAS SOMETHING TO DO WITH THE JUMBLE® PICTURE.

Unscramble the Jumbles, one letter to each square, to form words. Each word will be represented in the picture on the previous page.

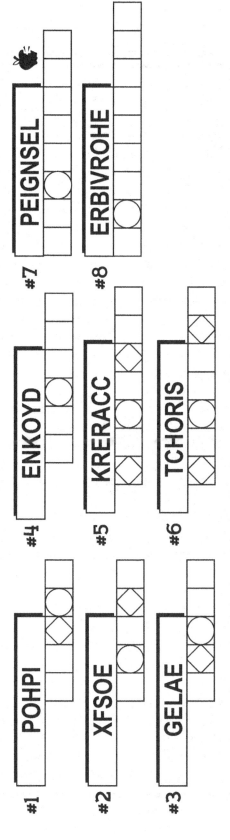

#1 POHPI

#2 XFSOE

#3 GELAE

#4 ENKOYD

#5 KRERACC

#6 TCHORIS

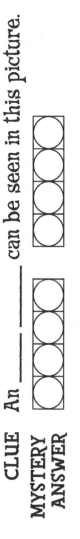

#7 PEIGNSEL

#8 ERBIVROHE

Arrange the circled letters to solve the mystery answer. Clues to the mystery answer can be found somewhere in the picture on the previous page.

CLUE   An _____ can be seen in this picture.

MYSTERY ANSWER

Arrange the diamonded letters to solve the mystery object. This object appears in the picture on the previous page but not in the previous picture(s) in the series.

Object that's been added to this picture

155

JUMBLE® #73
SEE&SEARCH™

JUMBLE®
SEE & SEARCH™

What's Different?

EVERY ANSWER HAS SOMETHING TO DO WITH THE JUMBLE® PICTURE.

Unscramble the Jumbles, one letter to each square, to form words. Each word will be represented in the picture on the previous page.

#1 VEAC

#2 MEULP

#3 RAZBE

#4 ROBRU

#5 ONBAOB

#6 NOTYHP

#7 EFIRAFG

#8 RAKNAOGO

Arrange the circled letters to solve the mystery answer. Clues to the mystery answer can be found somewhere in the picture on the previous page.

CLUE   A _____ can be seen in this picture.

MYSTERY ANSWER

Arrange the diamonded letters to solve the mystery object. This object appears in the picture on the previous page but not in the previous picture(s) in the series.

Object that's been added to this picture

157

Unscramble the Jumbles, one letter to
each square, to form words. Each word
will be represented in the picture on the
previous page.

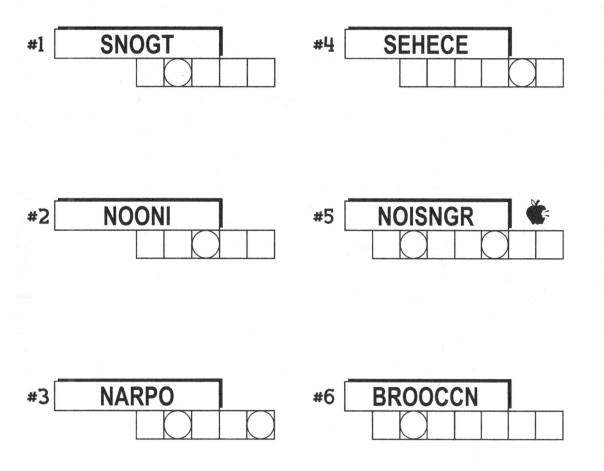

#1 SNOGT

#4 SEHECE

#2 NOONI

#5 NOISNGR

#3 NARPO

#6 BROOCCN

Arrange the circled letters to solve the mystery answer. Clues to the mystery answer can be found
somewhere in the picture on the previous page.

CLUE   One lady can be seen giving these to the other in this picture.

MYSTERY
ANSWER

Unscramble the Jumbles, one letter to each square, to form words. Each word will be represented in the picture on the previous page.

#1 **RATY**

#2 **UMSEO**

#3 **GIFTH**

#5 **PEARSG**

#5 **SNUTIEL**

#6 **LOAHDYI**

#7 **ROAPUCBD**

#8 **ROHUMSOM**

Arrange the circled letters to solve the mystery answer. Clues to the mystery answer can be found somewhere in the picture on the previous page.

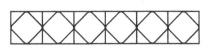

CLUE Three people can be seen _____ in this picture.

MYSTERY
ANSWER

Arrange the diamonded letters to solve the mystery object. This object appears in the picture on the previous page but not in the previous picture(s) in the series.

Object that's
been added
to this picture

161

162

Unscramble the Jumbles, one letter to
each square, to form words. Each word
will be represented in the picture on the
previous page.

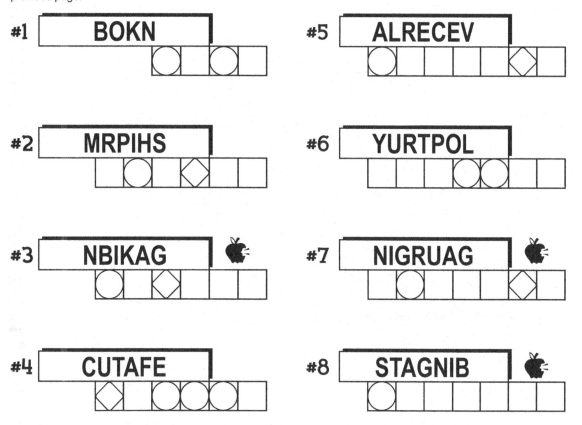

#1 **BOKN**

#5 **ALRECEV**

#2 **MRPIHS**

#6 **YURTPOL**

#3 **NBIKAG**

#7 **NIGRUAG**

#4 **CUTAFE**

#8 **STAGNIB**

Arrange the circled letters to solve the mystery answer. Clues to the mystery answer can be found
somewhere in the picture on the previous page.

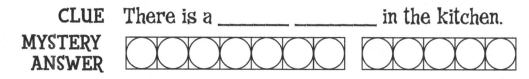

CLUE   There is a _____ _____ in the kitchen.

MYSTERY
ANSWER

Arrange the diamonded letters to solve the mystery object. This object appears in the picture on the
previous page but not in the previous picture(s) in the series.

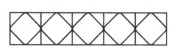

Object that's
been added
to this picture

164

EVERY ANSWER HAS
SOMETHING TO DO WITH
THE JUMBLE® PICTURE.

Unscramble the Jumbles, one letter to
each square, to form words. Each word
will be represented in the picture on the
previous page.

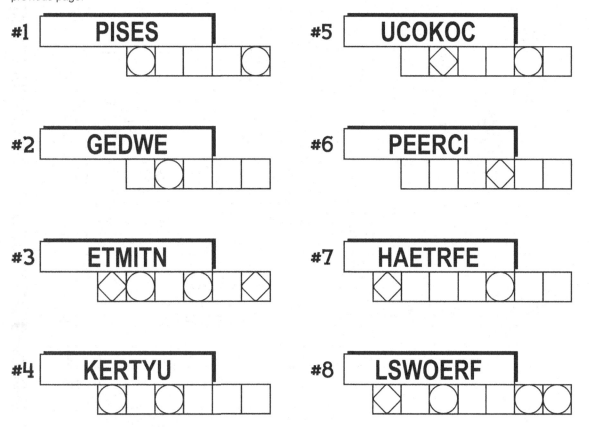

#1 PISES

#2 GEDWE

#3 ETMITN

#4 KERTYU

#5 UCOKOC

#6 PEERCI

#7 HAETRFE

#8 LSWOERF

Arrange the circled letters to solve the mystery answer. Clues to the mystery answer can be found
somewhere in the picture on the previous page.

CLUE   The grandfather didn't know how to tell these.

MYSTERY
ANSWER

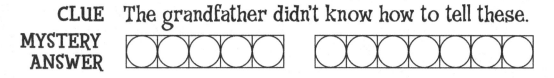

Arrange the diamonded letters to solve the mystery object. This object appears in the picture on the
previous page but not in the previous picture(s) in the series.

Object that's
been added
to this picture

Unscramble the Jumbles, one letter to
each square, to form words. Each word
will be represented in the picture on the
previous page.

#1 KAMS

#4 CROCES

#2 SAEBS

#5 GRINRE

#3 NUMDO

#6 NIKSGI

Arrange the circled letters to solve the mystery answer. Clues to the mystery answer can be found
somewhere in the picture on the previous page.

CLUE   The injured badminton player sees these.

MYSTERY
ANSWER

EVERY ANSWER HAS
SOMETHING TO DO WITH
THE JUMBLE® PICTURE.

Unscramble the Jumbles, one letter to
each square, to form words. Each word
will be represented in the picture on the
previous page.

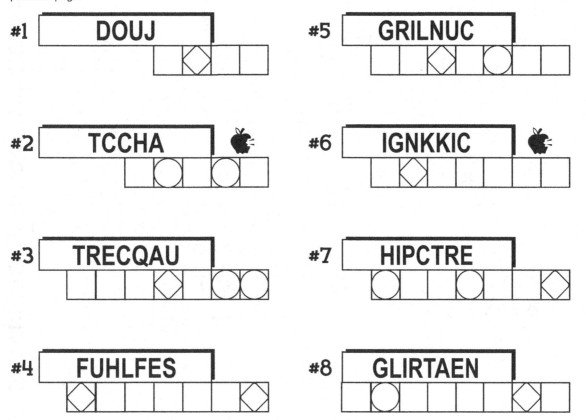

#1 DOUJ

#5 GRILNUC

#2 TCCHA

#6 IGNKKIC

#3 TRECQAU

#7 HIPCTRE

#4 FUHLFES

#8 GLIRTAEN

Arrange the circled letters to solve the mystery answer. Clues to the mystery answer can be found
somewhere in the picture on the previous page.

CLUE   A lot of _____ is going on in this picture.

MYSTERY
ANSWER

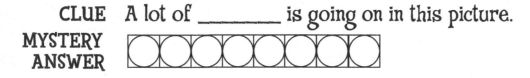

Arrange the diamonded letters to solve the mystery object. This object appears in the picture on the
previous page but not in the previous picture(s) in the series.

Object that's
been added
to this picture

EVERY ANSWER HAS SOMETHING TO DO WITH THE JUMBLE PICTURE.

Unscramble the Jumbles, one letter to each square, to form words. Each word will be represented in the picture on the previous page.

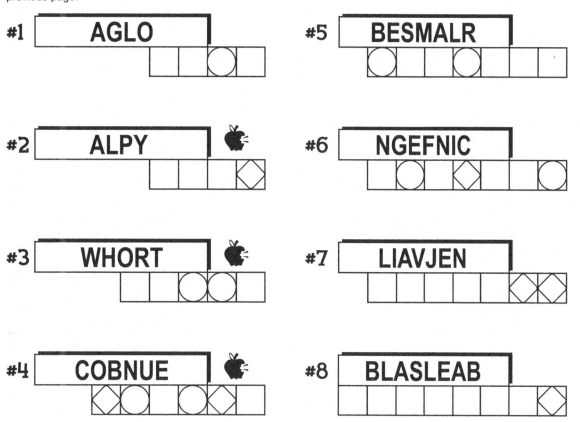

#1 AGLO

#2 ALPY

#3 WHORT

#4 COBNUE

#5 BESMALR

#6 NGEFNIC

#7 LIAVJEN

#8 BLASLEAB

Arrange the circled letters to solve the mystery answer. Clues to the mystery answer can be found somewhere in the picture on the previous page.

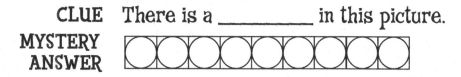

CLUE There is a _____ in this picture.

MYSTERY ANSWER

Arrange the diamonded letters to solve the mystery object. This object appears in the picture on the previous page but not in the previous picture(s) in the series.

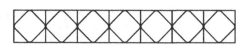

Object that's been added to this picture

What's Different?

JUMBLE.
SEE&SEARCH.

Unscramble the Jumbles, one letter to
each square, to form words. Each word
will be represented in the picture on the
previous page.

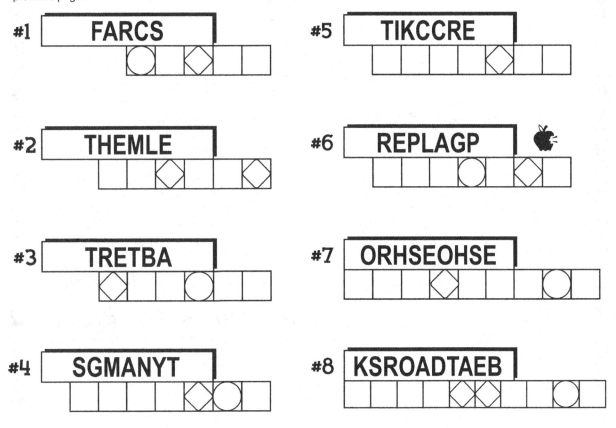

#1 FARCS

#2 THEMLE

#3 TRETBA

#4 SGMANYT

#5 TIKCCRE

#6 REPLAGP

#7 ORHSEOHSE

#8 KSROADTAEB

Arrange the circled letters to solve the mystery answer. Clues to the mystery answer can be found
somewhere in the picture on the previous page.

CLUE   There are a lot of _____ in this picture.

MYSTERY
ANSWER

Arrange the diamonded letters to solve the mystery object. This object appears in the picture on the
previous page but not in the previous picture(s) in the series.

Object that's
been added
to this picture

173

EVERY ANSWER HAS
SOMETHING TO DO WITH
THE JUMBLE® PICTURE.

Unscramble the Jumbles, one letter to
each square, to form words. Each word
will be represented in the picture on the
previous page.

#1 DAYR

#5 GLAVRU

#2 LEICS

#6 IPMNALCO

#3 BTIABR

#7 KASPESRE

#4 ASUPMC

Arrange the circled letters to solve the mystery answer. Clues to the mystery answer can be found
somewhere in the picture on the previous page.

CLUE   This is where you may find this scene.

MYSTERY
ANSWER   AT A

EVERY ANSWER HAS
SOMETHING TO DO WITH
THE JUMBLE PICTURE.

What's Different?

JUMBLE
SEE&SEARCH ™

Unscramble the Jumbles, one letter to
each square, to form words. Each word
will be represented in the picture on the
previous page.

#1 VOEN

#2 PMLBI

#3 RUAECS

#4 ROCTAR

#5 BCPUHA

#6 YEMNHCI

#7 TUSDENST

#8 QNUANENIM

Arrange the circled letters to solve the mystery answer. Clues to the mystery answer can be found
somewhere in the picture on the previous page.

CLUE   Believe it or not, there are fourteen _____ in this picture.

MYSTERY
ANSWER

Arrange the diamonded letters to solve the mystery object. This object appears in the picture on the
previous page but not in the previous picture(s) in the series.

Object that's
been added
to this picture

177

EVERY ANSWER HAS
SOMETHING TO DO WITH
THE JUMBLE® PICTURE.

Unscramble the Jumbles, one letter to
each square, to form words. Each word
will be represented in the picture on the
previous page.

#1 SONIY

#5 DSDARES

#2 THIGL

#6 RODYAWO

#3 LOTUET

#7 ERDMOFE

#4 KRENOB

#8 TRUPMECO

Arrange the circled letters to solve the mystery answer. Clues to the mystery answer can be found
somewhere in the picture on the previous page.

CLUE   Many of these people could be called this.

MYSTERY
ANSWER

Arrange the diamonded letters to solve the mystery object. This object appears in the picture on the
previous page but not in the previous picture(s) in the series.

Object that's
been added
to this picture

179

EVERY ANSWER HAS
SOMETHING TO DO WITH
THE JUMBLE® PICTURE.

Unscramble the Jumbles, one letter to
each square, to form words. Each word
will be represented in the picture on the
previous page.

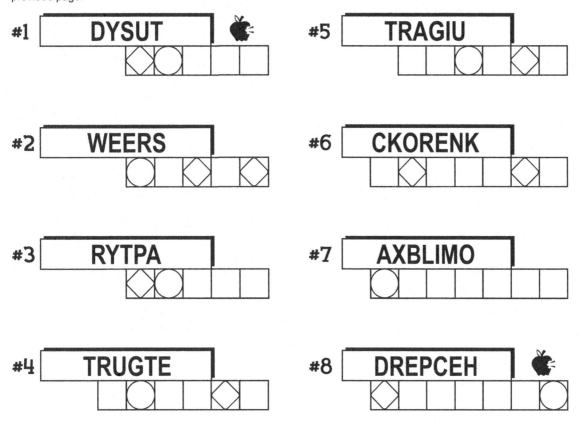

#1 DYSUT

#2 WEERS

#3 RYTPA

#4 TRUGTE

#5 TRAGIU

#6 CKORENK

#7 AXBLIMO

#8 DREPCEH

Arrange the circled letters to solve the mystery answer. Clues to the mystery answer can be found
somewhere in the picture on the previous page.

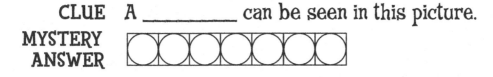

CLUE   A _____ can be seen in this picture.

MYSTERY
ANSWER

Arrange the diamonded letters to solve the mystery object. This object appears in the picture on the
previous page but not in the previous picture(s) in the series.

Object that's
been added
to this picture

1. **Jumbles:** #1 YELL #2 CORD #3 DESK #4 LAZY #5 LUNCH #6 DRINK #7 POLISH #8 CABINET
   Answer: The one thing the slacking secretary could file— HER NAILS
   Mystery Object: STAPLER

2. **Jumbles:** #1 TUBE #2 RULER #3 BOXES #4 CHARGE #5 PACKAGE #6 MAILMAN #7 ENVELOPE #8 DISPENSER
   Answer: What the sale at the post office caused—A STAMPEDE
   Mystery Verb: PANIC

3. **Jumbles:** #1 TRASH #2 RELAX #3 MOWER #4 CHECKS #5 VACUUM #6 RECLINE #7 CURTAIN #8 PERSPIRE #9 PAINTING #10 SPRINKLER
   Answer: Completing all of the chores made him feel this way— LISTLESS
   Mystery Objects: HAMMER AND NAILS

4. **Jumbles:** #1 KING #2 BAND #3 CREST #4 NOBLE #5 CROWN #6 SHIELD #7 UKULELE #8 HIGHNESS #9 TAPESTRY
   Answer: Where the royal guards went to relax— AT A KNIGHT CLUB
   Mystery Object: ROUND TABLE

5. **Jumbles:** #1 NECK #2 FLUTE #3 BANJO #4 KOOKY #5 STAND #6 DISPLAY #7 MUSICIAN #8 SAXOPHONE #9 INSTRUMENT
   Answer: The guitarist was asked to leave because he was this— TOO PICKY
   Mystery Object: MUSIC STORE

6. **Jumbles:** #1 MASK #2 FANS #3 CHEER #4 DOCTOR #5 SCALPEL #6 POPCORN #7 OPERATE #8 UNIFORM #9 HOSPITAL
   Answer: The ex-ball player did this when he became a surgeon—MADE THE CUT
   Mystery Object: PATIENT

7. **Jumbles:** #1 MILK #2 BULL #3 BRAND #4 CHURN #5 BOTTLE #6 HOOVES #7 HOLLER #8 HAYSTACK
   Answer: The cow wanted a divorce because she had this— A BUM STEER
   Mystery Object: BARN DOOR

8. **Jumbles:** #1 PIANO #2 SKULL #3 EYELID #4 SATURN #5 POLICE #6 ANTENNA #7 BARKING #8 SKYLINE #9 SATELLITE
   Answer: The lost space creature felt this way—ALIENATED
   Mystery Object: OUTER SPACE

9. **Jumbles:** #1 DUCK #2 WATER #3 GLOBE #4 PLUNGE #5 BANNER #6 STADIUM #7 DOLPHIN #8 SURPRISED
   Answer: What the novice Olympic diver made—A BIG SPLASH
   Mystery Object: CANNONBALL

10. **Jumbles:** #1 CART #2 BUMP #3 WHEEL #4 ROBOT #5 PRETZEL #6 ADDRESS #7 HYDRANT #8 DOORWAY
    Answer: They thought the street vendor was this—PUSHY
    Mystery Object: MAN HOLE

11. **Jumbles:** #1 TUBE #2 PARK #3 WAGON #4 WATCH #5 SHADOW #6 ABSURD #7 BALANCE #8 UMBRELLA
    Answer: The street artist knew how to do this— DRAW A CROWD
    Mystery Object: BERET

12. **Jumbles:** #1 FILM #2 PLAN #3 AVAIL #4 MOUSE #5 SOCKET #6 NEEDLE #7 SPRING #8 GENIUS #9 HAMMER #10 BATTERY
    Answer: Inventing the light bulb guaranteed Edison one— A BRIGHT FUTURE
    Mystery Objects: INVENTIONS

13. **Jumbles:** #1 WAVE #2 GULL #3 FANCY #4 MIRROR #5 WAITER #6 LOTION #7 LOUNGE #8 WORSHIP #9 PORPOISE
    Answer: A conceited person's vacation can be this— AN EGO TRIP
    Mystery Object: REFLECTION

14. **Jumbles:** #1 FLAG #2 PILE #3 FISHY #4 NOZZLE #5 BRIDGE #6 RACCOON #7 STENCH #8 SNEAKERS #9 TRASH CAN #10 SMOKESTACK
    Answer: The view at the dump was this—BREATH TAKING
    Mystery Object: RODENT

15. **Jumbles:** #1 BOOM #2 COMB #3 ALLEY #4 FAINT #5 GUTTER #6 WAXING #7 POWDER #8 FRAMES #9 BEVERAGE #10 DELIVERY
    Answer: She was this when he said he loved her— BOWLED OVER
    Mystery Object: PERFECT GAME

16. **Jumbles:** #1 BOOT #2 ICICLE #3 BUCKLE #4 HELPER #5 AFRAID #6 SNOWMAN #7 MITTENS #8 ORNAMENT #9 REINDEER #10 DIRECTION
    Answer: The child who is afraid of Santa is this— CLAUSTROPHOBIC
    Mystery Object: ANTLERS

17. **Jumbles:** #1 FUME #2 RAILS #3 RAPID #4 SIXTY #5 SHEEP #6 RABBIT #7 ISLAND #8 TRACTOR #9 TORTOISE #10 CROSSING
    Answer: A train conductor's favorite drink—EXPRESSO
    Mystery Object: STREAMLINER

18. **Jumbles:** #1 POND #2 ARCH #3 WILLOW #4 CANVAS #5 PADDLE #6 TURTLE #7 WALKWAY #8 SANDALS
    Answer: Blue and green are considered these— WATERCOLORS
    Mystery Object: LANDSCAPE

19. **Jumbles:** #1 HAWK #2 FENCE #3 MONEY #4 QUILT #5 FIELDS #6 GOURDS #7 COUNTRY #8 HARVEST #9 UNHAPPY #10 CUCUMBER
    Answer: The successful farmer did this to his competition— SQUASHED THEM
    Mystery Object: FARM HOUSE

20. **Jumbles:** #1 DADDY #2 PARROT #3 WREATH #4 MOTHER #5 ROCKER #6 HEARTH #7 COOKIES #8 PORTRAIT #9 LOLLIPOP #10 MAGAZINE
    Answer: The grandchildren considered grandma's to be this— HOME SWEET HOME
    Mystery Object: CHILDHOOD

21. **Jumbles:** #1 CLUBS #2 MOUND #3 TOWEL #4 SPLASH #5 BUNKER #6 SPIKES #7 ADVICE #8 SHRUBS #9 SWINGING #10 DISTANCE
    Answer: The persistent golfer had this—DRIVING AMBITION
    Mystery Object: LINKS COURSE

22. **Jumbles:** #1 MIXES #2 DRUNK #3 WRECK #4 JEWELS #5 BOTTOM #6 SEAWEED #7 MARTINI #8 SEASHELL
    Answer: The fish failed bartender school because his drinks were this—WATERED DOWN
    Mystery Object: SUBMARINE

23. **Jumbles:** #1 CRAB #2 CHILL #3 PLUME #4 BAMBOO #5 OYSTER #6 GREENS #7 COUPLE #8 SKEWER #9 ERUPTION
    Answer: A honeymoon salad is this—LETTUCE ALONE
    Mystery Object: SHORELINE

24. **Jumbles:** #1 YOLK #2 KAZOO #3 DOLLY #4 BLUSH #5 PUPPET #6 CRAYON #7 WHISTLE #8 NOSTRIL #9 ASHAMED #10 SHELVES
    Answer: The naked toy was this—A TEDDY BARE
    Mystery Object: TRINKETS

25. **Jumbles:** #1 DESK #2 SMOKE #3 PENCIL #4 BASKET #5 DISMAY #6 COBWEB #7 TYPING #8 MONITOR #9 CHEVRON #10 KEYBOARD #11 BULLETIN
Answer #1: A computer programmer's favorite snack— MICRO CHIPS
Answer #2: A sign that a computer is getting old— MEMORY LOSS

26. **Jumbles:** #1 GLOVE #2 HATCH #3 ORBIT #4 WORLD #5 WRENCH #6 PLANETS #7 UNIFORM #8 FLOATING #9 CONTROLS #10 EXPERIMENT
Answer #1: The astronauts used one to warm up— A SPACE HEATER
Answer #2: An astronaut's favorite drink—MOONSHINE

27. **Jumbles:** #1 CYCLE #2 PHONE #3 CRUISE #4 TRAVEL #5 STATUE #6 CAMERA #7 PODIUM #8 BLAZER #9 VACATION #10 SCISSORS #11 SPINNERS #12 MICROPHONE
Answer #1: The game show player that would not stop talking was—AN INCESSANT CONTESTANT
Answer #2: The game show players tried to win this— A PRIZED POSSESSION

28. **Jumbles:** #1 BELL #2 PILLOW #3 FAUCET #4 BUCKET #5 BOVINE #6 MASSAGE #7 PUMPING #8 DISTILL #9 CHICKEN #10 SPEAKER #11 BUTTERFLY
Answer #1: A pampered cow gives this—SPOILED MILK
Answer #2: A cow's favorite drink—BUTTERSCOTCH

29. **Jumbles:** #1 BONES #2 WALLET #3 ACHING #4 NEEDLE #5 OFFICE #6 CURTAIN #7 DIPLOMA #8 PROFILE #9 EXAMINE #10 SKELETON
Answer #1: The vampire doctor's favorite test—BLOOD COUNT
Answer #2: The doctor was doing this when he offered free services—TREATING

30. **Jumbles:** #1 SOAP #2 BACON #3 WATER #4 LOVING #5 KITTEN #6 SOAKED #7 BUFFET #8 SLIPPERS #9 DOCUMENT #10 THANKFUL
Answer #1: The businessman wore one in the tub— A BATHING SUIT
Answer #2: The children gave their sleeping mother this on her birthday—A BED SPREAD

31. **Jumbles:** #1 DISH #2 WHALE #3 GROOM #4 GOOSE #5 ARROW #6 TUXEDO #7 BEARER #8 STORMY #9 CORSAGE #10 BOUNCED #11 LIGHTNING
Answer #1: The bride wanted this before nuptials, not during— A WEDDING SHOWER
Answer #2: The successful husband always got in these last words—YES DEAR

32. **Jumbles:** #1 GOWN #2 SMOKY #3 VISOR #4 CUFFED #5 BONNET #6 DISPLAY #7 HANGERS #8 TIGHTEN #9 EYELASH #10 CLOTHIER
Answer #1: Searching for the perfect new ones can be one— A TRYING TIME
Answer #2: A temperamental tailor can do this to his customers—GIVE THEM FITS

33. **Jumbles:** #1 FLAPS #2 SNAKE #3 COYOTE #4 HOTDOG #5 HELMET #6 AFRAID #7 HOWLING #8 COOKING #9 OUTDOORS #10 SCORPION
Answer #1: What the fireman's ex-girlfriend was— AN OLD FLAME
Answer #2: The campers got engaged near one— A RING OF FIRE

34. **Jumbles:** #1 IRON #2 STAMP #3 SUNDAE #4 WINDOW #5 BORDER #6 INFLAME #7 CLOTHES #8 FLAMINGO #9 HEADLINE #10 NEWSPAPER
Answer #1: He became one after telling his wife how to drive— A PEDESTRIAN
Answer #2: Women get more love letters from him than anyone else—THE MAILMAN

35. **Jumbles:** #1 VAULT #2 THIEF #3 BROOM #4 CHANGE #5 WALKER #6 COFFEE #7 PYRAMID #8 BLENDER #9 NECKLACE #10 STEALING
Answer #1: The artistic investment banker show his off— PORTFOLIO
Answer #2: When the cashier reported her coworker she was this—A BANK TELLER

36. **Jumbles:** #1 TAXI #2 BOOTS #3 TOWEL #4 COWBOY #5 FAUCET #6 WAXING #7 BUCKLE #8 OCTAGON #9 PERSPIRE #10 POLISHED
Answer #1: The top car washer set this type of example— A SHINING ONE
Answer #2: The car-wash worker was this after a long day— WIPED OUT

37. **Jumbles:** #1 GLASS #2 BOXED #3 WATCH #4 SWITCH #5 BROKEN #6 STAPLER #7 BOOKLET #8 FIXTURE #9 MANAGER #10 CONSTRUCT
Answer #1: Making instruction books can be considered this— MANUAL LABOR
Answer #2: Checking the lamp instruction book was this— LIGHT READING

38. **Jumbles:** #1 LONER #2 COUCH #3 MINGLE #4 BLOUSE #5 CHATTY #6 NAPKIN #7 ATTACK #8 BUTTON #9 HEADSET #10 CRACKED
Answer #1: What the telemarketer considered her job to be— A CALLING
Answer #2: What the telemarketer made at the party— A CONNECTION

39. **Jumbles:** #1 HOOD #2 TRASH #3 PAPER #4 RADIO #5 TUNNEL #6 TRACKS #7 LIZARD #8 CABOOSE #9 COMMUTE #10 WARNING #11 STATION
Answer #1: The forgetful businessman lost this— HIS TRAIN OF THOUGHT
Answer #2: This is how the lifeguard got to work— A CAR POOL

40. **Jumbles:** #1 MONEY #2 ANGRY #3 RATTLE #4 PURSES #5 FITTED #6 BOW TIE #7 PACIFIER #8 BILLFOLD #9 CHARGING #10 ESCALATOR
Answer #1: A purse can cause this—A GRAB BAG
Answer #2: Often harder than a diamond—PAYING FOR IT
Answer #3: His wife thought this about his new outfit— IT SUITED HIM

41. **Jumbles:** #1 DARTS #2 EMPTY #3 FRUIT #4 TATTOO #5 HELMET #6 DANCING #7 WHISKEY #8 SPILLED #9 POPCORN #10 BRACELET
Answer #1: This is a cure for dandruff—BALDNESS
Answer #2: Some people think a pub is good for this— WHAT ALES THEM
Answer #3: Even when he relaxed, the guitarist did this— FRETTED

42. **Jumbles:** #1 BENCH #2 TULIP #3 SWINGS #4 JOGGER #5 PIGEON #6 SELLING #7 HUSTLED #8 BACKPACK #9 FOUNTAIN #10 BLUSTERY
Answer #1: What emerged when the wind blew off his toupee— THE BALD TRUTH
Answer #2: The preacher exercised this way—RELIGIOUSLY
Answer #3: Good advice when offered a timepiece on the street—WATCH OUT

43. **Jumbles:** #1 WAVY #2 PHONE #3 STUMP #4 ACORN #5 RUDDER #6 TACKLE #7 COBWEB #8 LANDING #9 HOWLING #10 SQUIRREL
Answer #1: Word that they're biting can do this to a busy executive—LURE HIM AWAY
Answer #2: What the novice fisherman ended up with— A REEL PROBLEM
Answer #3: What the comedian duck was good at— WISE QUACKS

183

44. **Jumbles:** #1 DECK #2 WAGER #3 HANDLE #4 DOLLAR
#5 NUMBERS #6 BOUNCER #7 JACKPOT #8 SECURITY
#9 SPINNERS #10 GAMBLING
Answer #1: A night at the casino can be this—DICEY
Answer #2: What getting dealt four of a kind is—A GOOD DEAL
Answer #3: Why she tried the cigar—FOR A GAG

45. **Jumbles:** #1 EAGLE #2 DIVOT #3 WATER #4 IRONS
#5 BIRDIE #6 SWINGS #7 MANGLED #8 HANDCART
#9 PRACTICE #10 CLUBHOUSE
Answer #1: What it takes to be a winning golfer—
A LOT OF DRIVE
Answer #2: What balding jokes do after a while—
WEAR THIN
Answer #3: The golfer had to change socks because he had
this—A HOLE IN ONE

46. **Jumbles:** #1 WEEDS #2 BRIDLE #3 TONGUE #4 SADDLED
#5 BOVINES #6 INITIAL #7 VULTURE #8 FENCING
#9 APPROACH #10 BUTTERFLY
Answer #1: The pony had trouble speaking because he was
this—A LITTLE HORSE
Answer #2: Where the farmer went when he retired—
OUT TO PASTURE
Answer #3: The cow lying around was this—
GROUND BEEF

47. **Jumbles:** #1 PIGGY #2 DIRTY #3 FIELDS #4 BUCKET
#5 CHUBBY #6 TRACTOR #7 ROOFTOP #8 FLATTEN
#9 WAGGING #10 LAUGHING
Answer #1: The successful pig farmer was this—
FILTHY RICH
Answer #2: The spider that lived in the corn made one—
A COBWEB
Answer #3: The animals thought the farmer's jokes were this—
CORNY

48. **Jumbles:** #1 DRIP #2 WORM #3 TRUCK #4 DAISY
#5 BRANCH #6 BARREL #7 BEAVER #8 HOLLOW
#9 DIGGING #10 SQUIRREL
Answer #1: The gardener feels this at the end of the day—
BUSHED
Answer #2: The tree doctor got to this—
THE ROOT OF THE PROBLEM
Answer #3: The type of romance had by gardeners—BUDDING

49. **Jumbles:** #1 LIMBS #2 SKUNK #3 WOODS #4 BLIND
#5 TIPTOE #6 AFRAID #7 GRIZZLY #8 WHISTLE
#9 CHIPMUNK #10 PLAYBOOK
Answer #1: What the timid hunter did—PASSED THE BUCK
Answer #2: The coach followed one on his hunting trip—
A GAME PLAN
Answer #3: Not seeing any duck left the hunters feeling this
way—IN A FOWL MOOD

50. **Jumbles:** #1 PLANT #2 VIOLIN #3 CHEESE #4 DATING
#5 DOORKNOB #6 ENTRANCE #7 CRACKERS
#8 BEAUTIFUL #9 DRUMSTICK #10 SHELLFISH
Answer #1: The model ate off of FASHION plates.
Answer #2: A corkscrew might also be useful for opening this—
A CONVERSATION
Answer #3: What the gossip turned an earful into—
A MOUTHFUL

51. **Jumbles:** #1 SKULL #2 GRAVE #3 WITCH #4 SPOOKS
#5 PIRATE #6 HAUNTED #7 VULTURE #8 PUMPKIN
#9 MEDICINE #10 DOORSTEP
Answer #1: The ghost lived in one—A DEAD END
Answer #2: What the ghost considered his new girlfriend to
be—A SOUL MATE
Answer #3: What the doctor's son made on Halloween—
HOUSE CALLS

52. **Jumbles:** #1 BOTTLE #2 DAMPEN #3 ANCHOR #4 LOUNGE
#5 ICEBERG #6 OCTOPUS #7 PENGUIN #8 NECKLACE
#9 STRANDED #10 LIFEBOAT
Answer #1: What she hoped to find on her vacation ship—
A DREAMBOAT
Answer #2: What the captain of the vacation ship had—
CRUISE CONTROL
Answer #3: How the finely dressed passenger looked on the
ship—DECKED OUT

53. **Jumbles:** #1 GLASS #2 TROWEL #3 WINDOW #4 SHOVEL
#5 FATIGUE #6 HARD HAT #7 ACCIDENT #8 AMBITION
#9 CONSTRUCT #10 BLUEPRINT
Answer #1: A brick layer's ailment—FALLEN ARCHES
Answer #2: What the cement tycoon sought—
CONCRETE GAINS
Answer #3: What the ambitious architect had—
BIG PLANS

54. **Jumbles:** #1 PRIZE #2 CLOWN #3 SHIFTY #4 TICKET
#5 MIDWAY #6 BALLOON #7 COASTER #8 PELICAN
#9 TOSSING #10 CARNIVAL #11 BASEBALL
Answer #1: COTTON CANDY can be seen in this picture.
Answer #2: This was introduced in 1893 in Chicago—
THE FERRIS WHEEL

55. **Jumbles:** #1 BELT #2 LOUD #3 DIRTY #4 FIASCO
#5 CLOSET #6 DRUMMER #7 POSTERS #8 BROTHER
#9 JUMPING #10 SINGING #11 NOTEBOOK #12 BAREFOOT
Answer #1: Three of these can be seen in the picture—
FASHION DOLLS
Answer #2: This can be seen in the picture—
A GIRL'S ROOM

56. **Jumbles:** #1 ACTOR #2 USHER #3 BEAMS #4 CROWD
#5 MOVIES #6 CARPET #7 PREMIER #8 CHOPPER
#9 CAMERAS #10 BALLOONS #11 CHAUFFEUR
#12 AUTOGRAPH
Answer #1: There are three of these in the picture—
SPOTLIGHTS
Answer #2: There is one of these in the picture—POSTER

57. **Jumbles:** #1 SHOW #2 BUNNY #3 CHAOS #4 CHIMP
#5 PLAID #6 PIGEON #7 BANNER #8 HOOKED #9 CURTAIN
#10 SUITCASE #11 PERFORMER #12 SURPRISED
Answer #1: This is what the comic/magician considered his job
to be—FUNNY BUSINESS
Answer #2: There are several of these in the picture—
MAGIC TRICKS

58. **Jumbles:** #1 AISLE #2 GROOM #3 DRESS #4 BESTOW
#5 RUNNER #6 FEATHER #7 BOUQUET #8 TUXEDO
#9 SKYLINE #10 CEREMONY #11 FOOTPRINT
#12 OVERJOYED
Answer #1: You can see this in the picture—A SPECIAL DAY
Answer #2: You can see a pair of these in the picture—
LOVE BIRDS

59. **Jumbles:** #1 TROLL #2 FAIRY #3 QUEEN #4 GNOME
#5 DRAGON #6 KNIGHT #7 BALCONY #8 RAINBOW
#9 UNICORN #10 MAGICAL #11 FANTASY #12 MUSHROOM
Answer #1: There is this kind of plant in the picture—
A TREE OF HEARTS
Answer #2: You can see this place in the picture—
A MAGIC KINGDOM

60. **Jumbles:** #1 APPLE #2 BERET #3 CANVAS #4 ERASER
#5 STUDIO #6 SKETCH #7 SCULPT #8 MOHAWK
#9 SUBJECT #10 DISPLAY #11 PAINTER #12 PORTRAIT
Answer #1: You can find this in an art class—CREATIVITY
Answer #2: There is one of these in the picture—AN INSECT

61. **Jumbles:** #1 ALBUM #2 STRUM #3 CHORD #4 LAPTOP #5 RHYTHM #6 VOCALS #7 LYRICS #8 FIDDLE #9 CYMBALS #10 TRIANGLE #11 HARMONICA #12 RECORDING
Answer #1: There are six of these in this picture—MUSICIANS
Answer #2: There is one of these in this picture—A LEAD SINGER

62. **Jumbles:** #1 PANDA #2 SKIRT #3 GIFTS #4 HAPPY #5 TRACKS #6 FATHER #7 FAMILY #8 SANDBOX #9 CROOKED #10 SUNSHINE #11 JUMP ROPE #12 CELEBRATE
Answer #1: There is one of these in the picture—A BIRTHDAY BOY
Answer #2: There is one of these in this picture—A PHOTOGRAPH

63. **Jumbles:** #1 VENTS #2 COOLER #3 COPIER #4 RESUME #5 PUTTER #6 HIDING #7 BANANA #8 TYPING #9 STADIUM #10 NAPPING #11 JANITOR #12 PARACHUTE
Answer #1: There are eight of these in the picture—EMPLOYEES
Answer #2: This does not belong in the picture—A SEA SERPENT

64. **Jumbles:** #1 RUINS #2 WAVING #3 FRIEZE #4 SHRIMP #5 DIVING #6 SCHOOL #7 TRIDENT #8 BUBBLES #9 SNORKEL #10 HARPOON #11 ANEMONE #12 TREASURE
Answer #1: There is a SUBMARINE in the picture.
Answer #2: There is one of these swimming in the picture—A NAUTILUS

65. **Jumbles:** #1 TUBA #2 PLOW #3 KITTY #4 BENCH #5 CLOCK #6 HOCKEY #7 SHOVEL #8 HYDRANT #9 READING #10 SQUIRREL #11 SNOWBALL #12 AIRPLANE
Answer #1: There are a few different SIDEWALKS that can be seen in this picture.
Answer #2: A HOT DRINK can be seen in this picture.

66. **Jumbles:** #1 SOAP #2 TOWEL #3 RAZOR #4 POLISH #5 CABINET #6 PLUNGER #7 MEDICINE #8 TOOTHBRUSH
Answer: There are COTTON BALLS in this picture.

67. **Jumbles:** #1 FLAG #2 HAND #3 GHOST #4 ROLLER #5 CUTTER #6 SPATULA #7 SNOWMAN #8 AIRPLANE
Answer: There is a DOLLAR SIGN in this picture.

68. **Jumbles:** #1 HOOK #2 BROOM #3 MOWER #4 RADIO #5 BUCKET #6 SHOVEL #7 GAS CAN #8 COOLER #9 DRIVER
Answer: There are a lot of TOOL HANDLES in this picture.

69. **Jumbles:** #1 MASK #2 FLUTE #3 GLOVE #4 GUITAR #5 OUTLET #6 RACQUET #7 STRINGS #8 KEYBOARD #9 CASSETTE #10 BOOMERANG
Answer: There is a REMOTE CONTROL in this picture.

70. **Jumbles:** #1 IVORY #2 STORK #3 HYENA #4 POUCH #5 CAMEL #6 HABITAT #7 HOPPING #8 WHISKERS
Answer: A favorite snack at the zoo—ANIMAL CRACKERS

71. **Jumbles:** #1 JOEY #2 KOALA #3 LLAMA #4 MOOSE #5 PUFFIN #6 GOPHER #7 BEAGLE #8 STROLLER
Answer: Three FLIGHTLESS birds can be seen in this picture.
Added Object: GOLF BALL (near the golf hole next to the beaver)

72. **Jumbles:** #1 HIPPO #2 FOXES #3 EAGLE #4 DONKEY #5 CRACKER #6 OSTRICH #7 SLEEPING #8 HERBIVORE
Answer: An OPEN GATE can be seen in this picture.
Added Object: PEACOCK (in front of the open gate)

73. **Jumbles:** #1 CAVE #2 PLUME #3 ZEBRA #4 BURRO #5 BABOON #6 PYTHON #7 GIRAFFE #8 KANGAROO
Answer: A ZOO KEEPER can be seen in this picture.
Added Object: PEANUT (near the elephant's trunk)

74. **Jumbles:** #1 TONGS #2 ONION #3 APRON #4 CHEESE #5 SNORING #6 CORNCOB
Answer: One lady can be seen giving this to the other in this picture—OPINIONS

75. **Jumbles:** #1 TRAY #2 MOUSE #3 FIGHT #4 GRAPES #5 UTENSIL #6 HOLIDAY #7 CUPBOARD #8 MUSHROOM
Answer: Three people can be seen HIDING in this picture.
Added Object: BUTTER (on the table near the candle)

76. **Jumbles:** #1 KNOB #2 SHRIMP #3 BAKING #4 FAUCET #5 CLEAVER #6 POULTRY #7 ARGUING #8 BASTING
Answer: There is a BUTCHER BLOCK in this kitchen.
Added Object: KNIFE (on the table between the fork and plate)

77. **Jumbles:** #1 SPIES #2 WEDGE #3 MITTEN #4 TURKEY #5 CUCKOO #6 RECIPE #7 FEATHER #8 FLOWERS
Answer: The grandfather didn't know how to tell these—SHORT STORIES
Added Object: MUFFIN (in the oven below the turkey)

78. **Jumbles:** #1 MASK #2 BASES #3 MOUND #4 SOCCER #5 RINGER #6 SKIING
Answer: The injured badminton player sees these—BIRDIES

79. **Jumbles:** #1 JUDO #2 CATCH #3 RACQUET #4 SHUFFLE #5 CURLING #6 KICKING #7 PITCHER #8 TRIANGLE
Answer: A lot of PRACTICE is going on in this picture.
Added Object: SQUIRREL (behind the football player who is wearing a helmet)

80. **Jumbles:** #1 GOAL #2 PLAY #3 THROW #4 BOUNCE #5 MARBLES #6 FENCING #7 JAVELIN #8 BASEBALL
Answer: There is a BOOMERANG in this picture.
Added Object: BICYCLE (above the golf green)

81. **Jumbles:** #1 SCARF #2 HELMET #3 BATTER #4 GYMNAST #5 CRICKET #6 GRAPPLE #7 HORSESHOE #8 SKATEBOARD
Answer: There are a lot of SPORTS in this picture.
Added Object: BASKETBALL (behind the cricket player)

82. **Jumbles:** #1 YARD #2 SLICE #3 RABBIT #4 CAMPUS #5 VULGAR #6 COMPLAIN #7 SPEAKERS
Answer: This is where you may find this scene—AT A UNIVERSITY

83. **Jumbles:** #1 OVEN #2 BLIMP #3 SAUCER #4 CARROT #5 HUBCAP #6 CHIMNEY #7 STUDENTS #8 MANNEQUIN
Answer: Believe it or not, there are fourteen ADULTS in this picture.
Added Object: STEREO (above the oven near the guitar player)

84. **Jumbles:** #1 NOISY #2 LIGHT #3 OUTLET #4 BROKEN #5 ADDRESS #6 DOORWAY #7 FREEDOM #8 COMPUTER
Answer: Many of these people could be called this—HOUSEMATES
Added Object: FOOTBALL (beside the traffic light)

85. **Jumbles:** #1 STUDY #2 SEWER #3 PARTY #4 GUTTER #5 GUITAR #6 KNOCKER #7 MAILBOX #8 PERCHED
Answer: A STADIUM can be seen in this picture.
Added Object: NEWSPAPER (on the lawn near the keg)

JUMBLE SAMPLER ANSWERS

TV Jumble®:
Jumbles: GRANT LIVING MAGNUM DOLPHIN
Bonus: The show's first color broadcast was on March 13, 1967—THE GUIDING LIGHT

Jumble® Crosswords™:
Jumbles: #1A HITCHED #5A UNCAP #6A INEPT #7A INGESTS #1D HOUDINI #2D TACKING #3D HAPLESS #4D DONATES
Bonus: There are about 900,000 species of these—INSECTS

Jumble® BrainBusters™:
Jumbles: #1 HARVARD #2 NINETEEN #3 SOFTWARE #4 MICROSOFT #5 WEALTHIEST #6 WASHINGTON #7 BILLIONAIRE
Mystery Person: BILL GATES

185

JUMBLE® SAMPLERS

TV JUMBLE® by David L. Hoyt

Use the clues to help unscramble the four Jumbles, one letter to each square, to form four words.

Jumble® with a TV Twist!

RNTAG
Clue: M.R.'s boss

LIGNIV
Clue: Martha's existence

GNMAMU
Clue: T.S. role

PDINLHO
Clue: Bud's bud

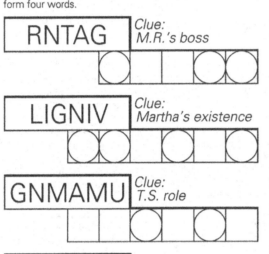

I remember this being on a lot when I was very young.

Bonus Clue: The show's first color broadcast was on March 13, 1967.

Then arrange the circled letters to form the bonus answer, as suggested by the above cartoon and bonus clue.

Bonus **THE** ⭕⭕⭕⭕⭕⭕⭕⭕ ⭕⭕⭕⭕⭕

JUMBLE® CROSSWORDS™

ACROSS

CLUE	ANSWER
1. Joined	THICDEH
5. Open	NPACU
6. Incompetent	PTINE
7. Eats	ESITNSG

DOWN

CLUE	ANSWER
1. Harry _____	UIOHIDN
2. Loose stitches	KAGITNC
3. Luckless	PSASHEL
4. Gives	NEDTASO

CLUE: There are about 900,000 species of these.

BONUS ⭕⭕⭕⭕⭕⭕⭕

How to play

Complete the crossword puzzle by looking at the clues and unscrambling the answers. When the puzzle is complete, unscramble the circled letters to solve the BONUS.

JUMBLE® SAMPLERS

JUMBLE® BrainBusters

MYSTERY PERSON

Unscramble the Jumbles, one letter to each square, to spell words that relate to the mystery person.

#1 RVHRADA

#2 ENIEENNT

#3 RWOTAESF

#4 FSICOORTM

#5 SHTELTIAEW

#6 GONWITNAHS

#7 ARNILIOIEBL

Arrange the circled letters to solve the mystery person.

Box of Clues

Use the clues below to help you solve the seven Jumbles.

- He was born in this U.S. state
- He attended this prestigious college
- Age at which he dropped out of college
- Adjective that describes his money situation
- This person is one many times over
- A product created by this person
- Company started by this person

MYSTERY PERSON

Need More Jumbles®?

Jumble® Books

More than 175 puzzles each!

Cowboy Jumble®
ISBN: 978-1-62937-355-3

Jammin' Jumble®
ISBN: 1-57243-844-4

Java Jumble®
ISBN: 978-1-60078-415-6

Jazzy Jumble®
ISBN: 978-1-57243-962-7

Jet Set Jumble®
ISBN: 978-1-60078-353-1

Joyful Jumble®
ISBN: 978-1-60078-079-0

Juke Joint Jumble®
ISBN: 978-1-60078-295-4

Jumble® Anniversary
ISBN: 987-1-62937-734-6

Jumble® at Work
ISBN: 1-57243-147-4

Jumble® Ballet
ISBN: 978-1-62937-616-5

Jumble® Birthday
ISBN: 978-1-62937-652-3

Jumble® Celebration
ISBN: 978-1-60078-134-6

Jumble® Circus
ISBN: 978-1-60078-739-3

Jumble® Cuisine
ISBN: 978-1-62937-735-3

Jumble® Drag Race
ISBN: 978-1-62937-483-3

Jumble® Ever After
ISBN: 978-1-62937-785-8

Jumble® Explorer
ISBN: 978-1-60078-854-3

Jumble® Explosion
ISBN: 978-1-60078-078-3

Jumble® Fever
ISBN: 1-57243-593-3

Jumble® Fiesta
ISBN: 1-57243-626-3

Jumble® Fun
ISBN: 1-57243-379-5

Jumble® Galaxy
ISBN: 978-1-60078-583-2

Jumble® Garden
ISBN: 978-1-62937-653-0

Jumble® Genius
ISBN: 1-57243-896-7

Jumble® Geography
ISBN: 978-1-62937-615-8

Jumble® Getaway
ISBN: 978-1-60078-547-4

Jumble® Gold
ISBN: 978-1-62937-354-6

Jumble® Grab Bag
ISBN: 1-57243-273-X

Jumble® Gymnastics
ISBN: 978-1-62937-306-5

Jumble® Jackpot
ISBN: 1-57243-897-5

Jumble® Jailbreak
ISBN: 978-1-62937-002-6

Jumble® Jambalaya
ISBN: 978-1-60078-294-7

Jumble® Jamboree
ISBN: 1-57243-696-4

Jumble® Jitterbug
ISBN: 978-1-60078-584-9

Jumble® Journey
ISBN: 978-1-62937-549-6

Jumble® Jubilation
ISBN: 978-1-62937-784-1

Jumble® Jubilee
ISBN: 1-57243-231-4

Jumble® Juggernaut
ISBN: 978-1-60078-026-4

Jumble® Junction
ISBN: 1-57243-380-9

Jumble® Jungle
ISBN: 978-1-57243-961-0

Jumble® Kingdom
ISBN: 978-1-62937-079-8

Jumble® Knockout
ISBN: 978-1-62937-078-1

Jumble® Madness
ISBN: 1-892049-24-4

Jumble® Magic
ISBN: 978-1-60078-795-9

Jumble® Marathon
ISBN: 978-1-60078-944-1

Jumble® Neighbor
ISBN: 978-1-62937-845-9

Jumble® Parachute
ISBN: 978-1-62937-548-9

Jumble® Safari
ISBN: 978-1-60078-675-4

Jumble® See & Search
ISBN: 1-57243-549-6

Jumble® See & Search 2
ISBN: 1-57243-734-0

Jumble® Sensation
ISBN: 978-1-60078-548-1

Jumble® Surprise
ISBN: 1-57243-320-5

Jumble® Symphony
ISBN: 978-1-62937-131-3

Jumble® Theater
ISBN: 978-1-62937-484-03

Jumble® University
ISBN: 978-1-62937-001-9

Jumble® Unleashed
ISBN: 978-1-62937-844-2

Jumble® Vacation
ISBN: 978-1-60078-796-6

Jumble® Wedding
ISBN: 978-1-62937-307-2

Jumble® Workout
ISBN: 978-1-60078-943-4

Jumpin' Jumble®
ISBN: 978-1-60078-027-1

Lunar Jumble®
ISBN: 978-1-60078-853-6

Monster Jumble®
ISBN: 978-1-62937-213-6

Mystic Jumble®
ISBN: 978-1-62937-130-6

Outer Space Jumble®
ISBN: 978-1-60078-416-3

Rainy Day Jumble®
ISBN: 978-1-60078-352-4

Ready, Set, Jumble®
ISBN: 978-1-60078-133-0

Rock 'n' Roll Jumble®
ISBN: 978-1-60078-674-7

Royal Jumble®
ISBN: 978-1-60078-738-6

Sports Jumble®
ISBN: 1-57243-113-X

Summer Fun Jumble®
ISBN: 1-57243-114-8

Touchdown Jumble®
ISBN: 978-1-62937-212-9

Travel Jumble®
ISBN: 1-57243-198-9

TV Jumble®
ISBN: 1-57243-461-9

Oversize Jumble® Books

More than 500 puzzles each!

Generous Jumble®
ISBN: 1-57243-385-X

Giant Jumble®
ISBN: 1-57243-349-3

Gigantic Jumble®
ISBN: 1-57243-426-0

Jumbo Jumble®
ISBN: 1-57243-314-0

The Very Best of Jumble® BrainBusters
ISBN: 1-57243-845-2

Jumble® Crosswords™

More than 175 puzzles each!

More Jumble® Crosswords™
ISBN: 1-57243-386-8

Jumble® Crosswords™ Jackpot
ISBN: 1-57243-615-8

Jumble® Crosswords™ Jamboree
ISBN: 1-57243-787-1

Jumble® BrainBusters™

More than 175 puzzles each!

Jumble® BrainBusters™
ISBN: 1-892049-28-7

Jumble® BrainBusters™ II
ISBN: 1-57243-424-4

Jumble® BrainBusters™ III
ISBN: 1-57243-463-5

Jumble® BrainBusters™ IV
ISBN: 1-57243-489-9

Jumble® BrainBusters™ 5
ISBN: 1-57243-548-8

Jumble® BrainBusters™ Bonanza
ISBN: 1-57243-616-6

Boggle™ BrainBusters™
ISBN: 1-57243-592-5

Boggle™ BrainBusters™ 2
ISBN: 1-57243-788-X

Jumble® BrainBusters™ Junior
ISBN: 1-892049-29-5

Jumble® BrainBusters™ Junior II
ISBN: 1-57243-425-2

Fun in the Sun with Jumble® BrainBusters™
ISBN: 1-57243-733-2